THE STILLNESS OF
TIME

TIME IS PRECIOUS

LIZ A ALEXANDER

authorHOUSE®

AuthorHouse™ UK
1663 Liberty Drive
Bloomington, IN 47403 USA
www.authorhouse.co.uk
Phone: 0800.197.4150

Author Photo by D&A Photography
www.da-photo.co.uk

Published by AuthorHouse   01/25/2019

ISBN: 978-1-7283-8332-3 (sc)
ISBN: 978-1-7283-8333-0 (hc)
ISBN: 978-1-7283-8331-6 (e)

Print information available on the last page.

This book is printed on acid-free paper.

"I am the wisest man alive, for I know one thing and that is that I know nothing". Socrates 469BC – 399BC a Greek Philosopher.

Dedicated to:

My children Emma, Thomas, James, Susanna and Benjamin.
Also all the very special people in my life and you all
know who you are. Last, but not least, all the very special
people whom I am destined to meet in the future

Introduction

Have you ever considered what time actually is? It's probably the only aspect of our lives we are in that we have absolutely no control over. We live with it every day but hardly spare it a thought; let alone a question. It is as familiar to us as breathing, so close to us that we don't even wonder what life would be like without it. Needless to say it is with us from the moment we are born until our lives are over. Yet we are swept along in a journey of time, hardly noticing why or how. When we are young we are oblivious of time as it exists in reality, survival is our main occupation. During middle age we are so busy being providers it seems we blink and it is gone, and we are left wondering what happened and asking the question "where did all those years go"? The latter years bring plenty of time to answer all those questions and more besides, only now what has passed, is past, never to return our way again. Perhaps by this time we will have made the most of every day or maybe not. The passing of time is so inconspicuous, almost unseen, silently working its magic minute by minute hour by hour that we are fooled by its stillness, unaware of its relentless endeavour to remain unobserved. Time is irreversible, unstoppable, and unpredictable - you cannot hold it in your hand - it just is. Think for a moment - it is only when it feels like it could be running out on us that we consider our connection with it. How many times have you heard the phrase 'Time is of the Essence' whatever does that really mean?

In the next few chapters I want to explore some elements of time as I perceive them to be. I hope they will provoke some interesting thoughts within you, thoughts which you may never have considered before. With the passing of time comes change if we can allow ourselves the time to stand still long enough to embrace it. Enjoy this journey through time. Let your thoughts and imaginings develop freely as you consider all of the different aspects of time past, present and future. I also hope the following pages will enable you to consider how you perceive time and its meaning in your life. To maybe ask the question am I aware of time passing by and if not why not? Do I take time out to make memories or is life just one big rush trying to keep up with the never-ending demands it throws at me? I challenge you to ponder for just a while about what the passing of time has meant to you so far, what it means to you now and how you might consider it in the future.

I hope by highlighting and reflecting on the different aspects of the passage of time and thus bringing it to your attention, it may cause you to consider where you have been on your journey and where you are now. Whether you manage your time, with anticipation and excitement or regret of what could have been. Perhaps by considering what has been you may find yourself searching for a new approach as to how you might spend your time in the future.

However, it takes you I know your time will not be wasted.

Contents

Chapter 1

The Measure of Time

It seems to me that we each measure time in different ways. Some of us see time as a reason to have to wait for things to happen or change, from which frustration can build and create annoyances and feelings of impatience. On the other hand, waiting, for others can bring joy and excitement by building expectations and a longing for what is to come. Dreaming and planning is sometimes needed to get the best from waiting even when hours seem like days and days seem like months.

I believe time is immeasurable, it moves at its own pace, stubbornly resisting any pressure to slow down or speed up. You cannot touch it, feel it or see it, it just is. Its' very existence is intangible and very inflexible. Scientists have proved time is measured by space and distance but I am in awe of this. Ancient cultures measured time by the sun, the moon, and the pattern of light and dark repeating itself, which is now day and night. Our existence in time is now measured by seconds, minutes and hours. We seem to be always chasing time as we know it, seemingly trying to make the most of what we can fit into a given hour or day. Unfortunately, we cannot stop the clock; it just goes on ticking, although we are thankfully mostly oblivious to the fact, as we live our busy lives.

Time is elusive, it avoids being trapped or caught up outside of itself and definitely does not pass the same way twice. Once it is has passed it is over, gone forever. It is also constant it does not change. How we experience it changes, but time stays the same. We owe it to ourselves to interpret the meaning of time in order to experience its' existence within ourselves to the best of our ability, as we travel along its' path. According to the experts, time does not stand still, so we are travelling along the journey of time whether we like it or not. My belief is that we can make the most of it while it is available to us whether good or bad, rich or poor, young or old, I could go on. How much we see paradise in our passing through time, remains unknown, so long as we try to look for it along the way. Avoid being misled by others' perception of time, or their impressions of how you live out yours. We can only live our own destiny, no one else's. How we appropriate the time we have depends a lot on who we are and where we are at any given opportunity, but rest assured we will only pass that way once. At the end of the day, we are only responsible for our own individual journey through time. No one else can be accountable for the way we spend our time, nor can anyone else tell us what is important or not on our journey.

Chapter 2

Living in the Rush of Time

We are on this planet for such a short time that the pace of life can absorb every ounce of our energy. From the time we are born and breathe out first breath, to the moment we die, we are being pushed and pulled in every direction known to man.

People in particular can be ruthless in their desire to succeed even though it may bring pain to those they love or a growing disregard for the needs of others. Their main objective being to satisfy an insatiable appetite to become bigger and better than they already are or to win the object of their desire, irrespective of the cost involved, and I do not mean money necessarily. "There is nothing wrong with success," you declare, "nor a competitive spirit!" "Not at all," I respond, but how long before something breaks down in the process. Juggling plates in the air is a very precarious occupation if you have ever tried it. Failure is eventually inevitable because it is unsustainable, due to the effort and cost involved. Likewise, an insatiable appetite, no matter what it is, can wear you down to a place where in the end you wonder how you got there and at what price. How long can you keep up the pace?

On the plus side, there is nothing wrong with ambition. Of course not, but how far will you let it drive you? To the edge? "Never," you answer. "How could it? I am in control of my own life and thus my own destiny." However, the relentless effort, sleepless nights and fallouts with those you love tell a different story. Where is the control now? Subtly, you eventually find yourself driven by a force not just from within but from every direction around you, and it never stops knocking at your door. Eventually, you have to answer and that is the sting, trapped in a never-ending cycle of demands far beyond what you ever imagined or designed for yourself. "I must take control" you shout. "But how?" Unable by now to see the wood for the trees, you feel consumed by others' expectations and manipulations that you find difficult to resist. No matter how hard you try or how fast you run they will always find a way to capture you. Life quickly takes on a different meaning. Too tired to argue or complain you find yourself giving in to almost every force or challenge that comes your way, as you are tossed and turned on a tide of demands, with little strength left to fight against them. Eventually, you have to ask yourself the question. "When or how did the control I so eagerly protected, slip so subtly though my fingers, and why was there no warning?" The questions go on but there seem to be no easy answers, especially to the question "Where is my control now?" Looking back, time for anything but the immediate was always in short supply. If there had been even a few opportunities to spend time considering the present they would have been quickly absorbed by distractions from all around. It would seem the cycle went on repeating itself until one day, all-be-it through different circumstances, you had to stop and think about the consequences. Consequences you could never have contemplated, but now are very real.

To define any particular reasons at this time would not necessarily be useful, but suffice to say that any situation that breaks down can leave us feeling confused and disappointed. Sadly, more often than not, the if-only thoughts and numerous questions come to play in our heads like a never-ending chorus. It is hard to drown them out, human nature being what it is, questions need answers. Having to stop and think was not what anyone would have preferred to plan, but it is not long before the realisation comes, this will be the only way forward in order to find any peace. Facing reality is difficult to do and requires us to be courageous and non-blaming. Trying to make sense of when or how will take time and effort to establish, but even so will be good preparation for any path we might choose to take in the future. You will always be in a position to choose, the ultimate choices being yours, at least while you still have the time to make them. How difficult or not that might be is another matter. Consuming activity in order to sustain any demanding lifestyle, is not easy to change, but perhaps by just considering the necessity to do something it might help to find a way. Maybe thought given to slowing down might be a starting point. Then as time allows, you can take stock of what has happened, and consider how it could have been avoided as you see it now. However, more often than not, life has a way of giving each of us a let-out clause if we really want one, but no doubt it will take thought, honesty and a few difficult decisions along the way.

One thing to be sure is that being driven by endless activity, has a way of not allowing us to see things the way they really are, and how they are affecting us and our significant others long term. Perhaps the better way forward is to be the one in the driving seat, the one who decides with assertiveness how much we are prepared to give up, in order to achieve our goals. Considering this before we start on our journey, may allow us the ability to be more discerning, when the pressures build and we will feel more able to say no. In fact, by being the driver rather than the driven, we take back control of managing our time the way we would like it to be and not the other way around. Perhaps more preparation might help to ascertain just how achievable our goals really are, whilst also trying to participate in everyday living, the main issue for success being to keep a balance in all things.

Chapter 3

Being in the Right Place at the Right Time.

Have you ever wondered what real effect this might have had or might have on your life in the future? Could it be that we unintentionally, subconsciously manage our lives in such a way that that's exactly where we find ourselves, or is it as some might think just a lucky break? I also consider the possibility that it could be construed as destiny over which I believe we have little or no control. I am certain that of the three suggestions, destiny is probably the least acceptable to most and regarded as a reason for matters that cannot be explained any other way. The human mind is not trained or developed to accept irregularities readily and in many cases not at all. Circumstances in which you find yourself, for whatever reason, are more easily accepted when we have some part in their construction. It requires a little more craziness to accept something which just occurs without any extra involvement from us, almost in fact, unexplainable.

I challenge you to think of the last time this happened to you. Did it occur to you to think 'that's strange, I don't remember putting anything in place for that to happen'. Perhaps you didn't even notice it was happening in which case the event would have gone unnoticed as anything but an inevitable happening. On the other hand, it may have set you thinking in the deeper recesses of your mind 'How did that happen and why?'. What created the circumstances to evolve in such a way to create the opportunity presented at that precise moment? I definitely believe in Destiny having quite a big role to play in every day living and certainly in my own life. There have been times when I have been left thinking, 'I could never have engineered this to happen in a million years, so what is going on?' So many times circumstances can dictate how we see ourselves in the future. Even though our expectations may not match the situation we find ourselves in, at any given moment our perceptions and situations can alter as time passes. Nothing can be set in stone especially where life is concerned. Each day can bring about a whole new canvas to work from and who knows what could happen to complete that? Time is no respecter of persons, as we all spend our time in different ways, hopefully ending up with some personal satisfaction. Being open to watching and waiting can have an immense impact on what ends up on our canvas of life. Is it possible, that impatience can block the natural progression of events and thus hinder our fulfilment and ultimate destiny, whatever that might be? Crossing paths which are not meant to be crossed, because we can't wait, could add such a different outcome to where we might have ended up. Once crossed it is difficult to know. Can we really shape our futures to such an extent that destiny cannot be involved even in a small way? Perhaps the controls we place on our-selves and the patterns we live everyday leave no space for destiny to have an influence, and even if it did it, could well be overlooked. Perhaps being in the right place at the right time can only exist where a space has been provided for it to operate. Maybe it is up to each of us to allow that to happen by exercising fewer restraints on our perception of what is going to be, rather than what might be if given the chance. Perhaps what could be true to say is we won't find out till we get there, wherever there is! Maybe we have more influence on our destiny or not than we realise. Can the role of destiny overrule the controls we place on our lives? In the wilder scheme of things, we subconsciously tend to avoid risks of any kind in order to feel safe and secure, in which case destiny might not get the opportunity to find fulfilment. Constant planning and organising our everyday lives brings security of a kind, but doesn't leave much room for deviation. Is it possible that the security we seek blinds us to options or choices which might have become available? For some that is really great because choices can seem threatening and better left for another day. However, for some the option of choice can be exactly what keeps living not just interesting, but exciting and unpredictable, adding spice to life and allowing a free spirit to operate with confidence and a sense of adventure.

How easy is it to slip into a mind-set of procrastination, finding excuses to convince ourselves that we are not ready for taking certain steps? Thinking it far better to stay where we are than risk falling at the first hurdle. I can understand this way of thinking and can empathise with those who engage in it, but I also know that putting off and avoiding possibilities can cause stagnation. If you think of a stagnating pool or lake, where no water flows in or out, it doesn't take long to realise that almost everything in it will eventually die and decay. Life in the form of living matter will eventually be extinguished because of the lack of fresh water and oxygen. Life cannot be sustained or move on where stagnation exists. The introduction of fresh, oxygenated water cleanses and brings life to an otherwise dead appearance. Is it possible this could happen to some of us in a greater or lesser degree by resisting new opportunities, refusing to open doors, or worse still not walking through open doors that might beckon us? Who can say this may have been the chance, in the journey we walk each day, for destiny to play its' part. Obviously, there will be a risk involved when we do anything unpredictable or spontaneous, but what's to lose, and maybe eventually gain. The point is, without a step into the unknown, we could perhaps stay exactly where we are and who knows for how long? Anticipation of change, prepares our minds for a clearer path to travel along, so that should an opportunity arise we will be able to see it and maybe respond by changing course and allowing destiny to have a say. Tennessee Williams said "To live is to change and not to change is to die". Strong words, but very meaningful, when you consider lost opportunities that might happen because we are too set in our ways. Focusing on the inevitable is ok, but what about chance or the hope of destiny playing a part in our lives too? Some might say that this is living too dangerously or on the edge and asking for trouble. I would dare to suggest that how do you know unless you try it? There is no such thing in anyone's life as an unimportant day, no matter what the outcome. If we are breathing we are alive, so that has to be something for many of us to rejoice about, don't you think?

Gail Sheehy, an American author, journalist and lecturer said "Growth demands a temporary surrender of security". So should we not be prepared to take a few little risks in order to grow at the same time? When facing the challenge of abseiling down a wall, a few years ago, I was almost completely beaten at the prospect of stepping off the wall into nothing! I knew I was in a safety harness and that there was someone at the top with me who had checked everything to make sure it was secure. In the brief moments I had before jumping off the wall, I tried to analyse what my problem was. I came to the conclusion that it was because I had never taken a step like this before and I was convinced that the safety harness might fail. I was determined not to panic and after a recheck I made the conscious decision to jump backwards. No one else could have convinced me to do this only myself, and the amazing feeling after taking that action cannot be put into words. Putting trust in the equipment surrounding me, and the sheer determination to prove that I could do it, overruled my fear of the unknown! The exhilaration I felt when I fell backwards was awesome. In a way I put my trust in destiny, in somewhat unusual circumstances, but none the less I could have walked away and denied myself the opportunity of that experience. Certainly by arranging every detail in our lives in order to be in control can, I am sure, unknowingly deny destiny a chance to operate to its' fullest extent. What do you think?

Chapter 4

Time is Ageless or is it?

The only measure of time that most of us know and are familiar with is seconds, minutes and hours, and of course days, weeks, months and years. We can look back in time as far as scientists can take us, but even going back that far does not seem to age time. When I see the sun, or a new or full moon or the North Star appear, as they must have done since time began, I ponder the thought that they could come under the category of ageless. It would seem they have always appeared in exactly the same way, no matter how many thousands of years have passed, and it is fascinating to think that they will continue to do so in the future for as long as they are allowed.

Looking back over history, and seeing what are known as the Natural Wonders of the World we can never quite be sure how long they have existed. Scientists and geologists have equipment to measure the age of such incredible, magnificent wonders, but it is difficult to imagine how they were in the beginning. We can only trust what the experts tell us. In the time we spend on this earth, compared to the possible hundreds or thousands of years it has taken for them to evolve, we can only imagine what changes might have taken place to make them what they appear to be now. If we were to call them, ageless it could be understandable, although it might not be accurate. They are aging all the time, but we are not able to see the process happening in our life time in any tangible way. The Egyptian pyramids stand tall and mighty, but over the thousands of years since coming into existence, they have been deteriorating little by little, day by day. They are not ageless as the Pharaohs intended for them to be, although how long they might take to disappear is impossible to gauge. If the Pharaohs were around to see them now they would probably be horrified!

Needless-to-say, I wonder how many folks stop to consider if time is ageless and even if they did, so what? It is understandable that we might all have a very different perspective on such an unusual concept. However, I am none the less curious. Time marches on regardless, irrespective of whether we consider it ageless or not, or whether we choose to care about such things. My curiosity aroused by the sheer pace of life and how much continuously changes around us every day. We imagine we are in control of so many parts of our lives, and yet as time slips through our fingers, the unquestionable fact is that the only thing that has aged is ourselves.

I have concluded that I have to accept time is ageless, but nothing around it is. Everything ages, no matter what we choose to think or do about it. We believe from today's amazing technology; even the galaxies are more than likely constantly changing. We, as temporary subjects are not aware of it here on earth because we are not here long enough to see it happening around us, nor can we focus that far into the distance. Who can measure agelessness, as we understand it? There will never be anyone old enough, who has lived long enough to answer that question with absolute certainty. However, suffice to say, that all the time our planet exists we human beings are aging against time, as we know it. Perhaps if we could fully understand the concept of aging, we would be more willing to engage in what the passing of time really means to each of us.

I am left with the notion that no matter where we look, what we find, or where we go, we are governed by the fact time has to be considered ageless. If not, we would have to accept the truth that there will come a time when it will naturally have to come to end! Then what?

Chapter 5

Do you have Time to Dream?

I have heard it said 'you have to have a dream to get up in the morning'. I am not sure where this saying comes from but I have heard it many times. How about you. Do you think dreaming is for fools or do you think we should always have time to dream? Some folk even go so far as to believe that dreams really do come true. I suggest that is something we can't judge till it happens to us personally. I like to think that having a dream is a bit like having hope. We give ourselves a plan to work towards and enjoy the working out of that plan always with the ambition to make our plan a success. The risk of failure is low on the scale of our thinking, even though it could happen, before our goal is accomplished. To enable the plan to exist, we have to start with a dream or vision, which little by little hopefully becomes a reality. I also believe that dreaming is the force behind being able to wait for things to occur that we have no control over. As our anticipation mounts we tend to visualise what we are waiting for, building a picture whilst dreaming about the end result. This is not magic, but a positive alternative to a frustrating situation we might experience whilst waiting and hoping for events to take shape.

Time spent dreaming is not always futile and a waste of time. It can be a comfort when it feels like time is standing still and all around us seems ineffective. As a mother, being pregnant was one of those occasions when there was a lot of time to do a lot of dreaming. Longing for the time to pass when the baby is ready to be born, can be like an eternity of waiting, but no amount of engineering will hasten that event. It is a well-known fact that most babies arrive when they are ready, and not a minute before. Somehow, dreaming about what is happening to us, and what our baby will look like or grow up to be, is a bit like a sedative. It woos us along each day and is necessary as we fall in love with the unseen, as yet unknown child we carry. We may even find ourselves daring to dream about how we will be as a parent, every thought being laden with excitement and apprehension mixed together at the same time. It's a good time to dream and very constructive, however long it takes!

Perhaps over time your experience has been that dreaming is a waste of time and only for those who want to escape reality. I am sure there are many who would agree with you, and possibly think the same way, but I challenge you to consider, what would you put in its' place? Life can be so hard for so many and what can be wrong in finding an alternative to motivate you to continue the fight. Perhaps dreaming makes us stronger for a while, giving us enough time to renew our energy to continue the battle we find ourselves in. Fighting for life must be exhausting and can be experienced at many levels. Dreaming can be the one thing that keeps us going, until we can effectively change our circumstances or win the war, whether it's inside or outside of ourselves. Some of our battles in life, would perhaps have been managed so much better, by having a chance to dream our way through some of the traumas! Dreaming can be a comfort to your soul when all else fails, and you find yourself in a very dark place, as we can all do. Sometimes people just don't do it for us at the time, as much as we or they would like to think they can, but that's ok. We will always need people in our lives, they are part of living every day.

Can you imagine a world without the capacity to dream? Many spend hours watching dramas and films that are completely built on fantasy, but somehow society finds that more acceptable. What do they actually represent but a chance to dream if only for a few hours? A lot of money is accumulated on the human need to imagine and fantasise about what can or might happen. We soak it up, loving every minute, whilst someone else's imagination transports us into another world. What is this if it's not dreaming? The only difference is we are being entertained by someone else's dreaming and not our own. The question has to be asked, is it not a waste of time as we escape the reality around us? Can it be more acceptable than spending time creating our own dreams and hopefully also enjoying every minute? I am not sure anyone is able to raise an eyebrow at someone else's time spent dreaming or fantasising their way through time, when they want or need to.

Dream away I say, so long as it doesn't do any one else any harm, enjoy it while you may, young or old, rich or poor we all do it. If it helps us cope with every day. Why not? We will always eventually be drawn back to reality whether reluctantly or willingly. Everyone is different, and that's a good thing, so live and let live is a good premise to work from. We can all have dreams, and dreams by their very nature can change unexpectedly. Perhaps we all need to make time to dream a little, if we never dream how will we ever have a dream come true?

Chapter 6

If we could Turn Back Time - would we?

Maybe a more meaningful, appropriate question might be, would we like to turn back time? Either way I am sure deep down, if we had a special button to press that might take us back in time if only for a few days, we might all be very tempted to use it now and again. After all there is a tendency to look back and extol times gone by and to reminisce on what used to be. The human mind has an amazing ability to forget the bad times and easily remember the good, thus perhaps giving us a slightly biased, rose coloured picture of the past. Maybe it's easier to live with the past if we are able to turn down the brightness a little and be more selective about what we choose to remember. None the less looking back, as we tend to put it, can also be a healthy thing to do, so long as we do it realistically. I am sure our memories could so easily play tricks on us, so that we might be more inclined to remember a slightly distorted picture of what actually was, if you know what I mean. We could be left unable to remember the truth of what we have experienced, but I am sure that when all things are considered, our minds might also be governed by our wills. Unless we have an illness or accident that stops that happening, if we want to remember we will, that is a reality.

Even so, I believe going back in time, all be it just in thought, is not always negative and that a lot can be accomplished for the present and the future by doing so. Let me explain. So much could be learnt as to how we might possibly redefine our future ambitions and decisions, as most would prefer to avoid any repeated mistakes or mishaps in the future. However, that would probably require an honest look at the past, scary as it might be, to grow and move on. Hiding from taking responsibility for our past mistakes or failures can only stunt our growth and keep us a prisoner in our own fears. Whereas, doing the opposite could be freeing and exhilarating, and we may even find ourselves wanting to embrace a whole new world of adventure enriched by self-discovery. I believe every perceived failure could be one step closer to success when looked at differently. We have the ability to exchange every past negative thought or action for something more positive and enlightening for the future if we choose to do so. Learning from what we or the world might consider to be failure, once replayed, can expose the full meaning and consequences of our situation then and what it means now. What can be gained by being so intent on staying stuck in the winter that we miss the spring and summer as it subtly passes by?

All through history time has forced changes to evolve often to the advantage of future societies, creating and inventing along its' way. Life itself has evolved through the passing of time, and it would seem futile to imagine turning back the clock to evaluate what has happened in the past in order to recreate the future. It could be seen as a bit like digging up a newly planted seed in order to see if it has started to germinate. In this respect we find ourselves in one aspect of time along our journey of life which we have little influence over, we are born and we die, what happens in between is what we can influence or not as the case maybe. Who knows what card we will have been dealt? As we live each day we will see our lives unfolding a bit like following a map, but we often don't know what we're going to find till we get there.

Will we ever be in a position to turn back the clock other than by regretful thoughts by wishing things could have been different. I am sure we are all guilty of entertaining that sort of wishful thinking, but it will probably end up being a depressing activity to indulge in. What has been is passed, never to return, moving on is a step that has to be taken if we want to enjoy our time now and in the future. Despite the probable feeling of a fear of the unknown we cannot healthily live back in time. It would eventually stunt our growth and I believe like a flower without water, it would eventually kill us. Living through our fears is a far more healthy occupation as we walk through our individual journeys of life.

Each and every day bears witness to the fact that all humans basically have similar fears, we are not alone. The only difference between us is that some are more able to share them, which of course can be really helpful. However, for those who find that difficult and for some impossible, it might seem easier to live in their fears rather than live through them. Going back in time, or rather making no effort to look ahead is easier. To reason that we are absolutely fine as we are is adequate for some. Pretending we are content with staying put, and not wanting to consider taking strides to move forward into the unknown is manageable and easily controlled. Engaging in thoughts of stepping out of our comfort zone can send some racing back to what they know, in order to restore the equilibrium of their security. They can easily adapt and be more content living in the past they know, which is not at all threatening. Perhaps some of us fear the unknown more than the possibility of stagnating and losing opportunities to advance and develop? However, once confronted what's the worst that could happen when trying to pursue the unchartered waters of life?

Time can be considered our friend, a friend who helps us to refocus on what could be, rather than what was. With time as a friend we can move on to greener pastures of hope and change. Each of us has a history of past experiences which can be built into another story for the future. Nothing is wasted with experience whether past or present. Each experience brings its' own rich tapestry of colours which, when intertwined together, enhance each other to create the most beautiful landscape without which the picture would not be complete.

Chapter 7

Living in the Moment Constantly Enriches Time.

What do you think living in the moment could mean? Is this a mind-set which we could all develop? Thinking about this for some while, I have managed to formulate some ideas. I consider living in the moment a very personal experience, which I am sure might require practice.

Perhaps the only way to begin might be to look at what definitely is not living in the moment. Procrastination, or constantly putting off anything or everything, is probably the complete opposite to living in the moment, eventually becoming a comfortable habit which is hard to break. Procrastination, has so many hidden agendas, which are none the less very real to each individual person. We can create endless corridors of reasons as to why we cannot do things now, some legitimate, some not, only we can justify our reasons. The problem is, living in the moment can require decisions and or actions to be taken at the said moment, in order to become a reality. Many hours can be spent tossing and turning thoughts over in our minds, trying to make decisions, only by the time we have found the answer we think we are looking for, we could have missed the moment!

Something to be considered here could be the need for affirmation. Trying to make decisions about anything in life can engage us in talking to many others in the hope of finding some sort of direction. I am not convinced that trying to avoid having to make a decision alone is always entirely helpful. On several occasions, when seeking another's advice, through reading or discussion, it has been made apparent to me that we are not always given the most accurate or honest appraisal. It doesn't mean that the person or persons are intentionally doing anything dishonest, it is far deeper than that. Even with the best will in the world, others can only usually advise us from the position of what they know and have experienced for themselves. Depending on where they were with their experience, and how they reacted to it at the time, will very much influence the support or answer they might give to another. All be it I am sure, with the best intention in the world, it would be difficult to give a detached viewpoint of objectivity.

It is normally human nature to want to help another to find peace in making decisions, or to deal with difficult circumstances, but unfortunately it is not always appropriate. There is a possibility that we can unintentionally advise others wrongly, or react negatively to their circumstances because of our own insecurities. Our personal reactions to bad experiences, can in their own way, create fears within ourselves which are very difficult to see at the time. Maybe, if we are unable to move on, we might sometimes find ourselves advising others not to move on either. Procrastinating, by running around trying to find answers to difficult questions from others, instead of stopping and seeing the reality of what we have to work with, can often leave us confused and frustrated. Of course it is not the case every time but it is good to know that this is a very real possibility. In high insight, what is more often needed, is to try to evaluate the situation for ourselves by realising the reality of our current circumstances, and considering what our options might be. There are those among us who might think that spending valuable moments doing this could be time consuming and unrealistic, but this is not always the case. Saving time by not running here, there, and everywhere, trying to find answers to difficulties and confusion, can be a welcome relief. Sometimes the answers we are seeking are possibly right where we are. A great lesson to learn might be, that the answers may lie in doing absolutely nothing, and spending more time contemplating the easily missed little things in order to see the bigger picture.

I sometimes wonder how many living in the moment opportunities I might have missed, although I know looking back will not reinvent them. However, it does remind me to stop and think about those I don't want to miss now or in the future. On reflection, chasing tomorrow can take up so much of our time we miss the experience of living in the moment. Constantly chasing rainbows, past experiences, disappointments, unfulfilled dreams or expectations can be a fruitless activity. Living and appreciating the present can bring contentment and fulfilment, that cannot be found anywhere else or in anything else. Every moment spent living in the now, enriches our dreams for the future and motivates us to never give up. Time spent with precious, living in the now moments, can bring a lasting joy and peace that can never be lost. It could be likened to the difference between a permanent tattoo and one painted on the body with temporary Henna. Time will eventually erase the fast, crazy lifestyles, which we are chasing and the memories of such will eventually fade into each other. However, living in the moment memories can never be erased and could enrich our lives in ways that we cannot imagine, which can and will be proved by the simple test of time.

Living in the moment is more than just a thought, it requires action, we can say yes or no, go left or right, who knows what we will choose, but inevitably a choice is needed. Do we sometimes follow our hearts and our instincts, or do we listen to our heads? It often comes down to following through to an unknown destiny without hesitation. Sometimes refusing to procrastinate can leave us free to start living in the moment. Why not give it a try?

Chapter 8

Time to Refocus

Life is full of surprises and amazement and of course also the opposite. Looking at obstacles with eyes of wonderment people might say is nothing less than impossible. Our immediate reaction might understandably be one of fright or flight, which I would say is normal for most of us. How we move on from the situation is what is important. Dealing with difficulties in ways that require maturity and confidence require time and experience, which is in short supply especially when we are still young and ambitious. Controlling our natural urges to fight or run is not easy at any time, but especially so when we are not so wise and also impatient. Living everyday teaches us many truths, and as we grow and learn, we slowly appreciate ways to proceed from struggling and disappointment. They say what doesn't kill us makes us stronger, but at the time not many of us can see the wisdom or value in those few words. However, our way of overcoming trials, by also seeing good in such things, I think could be a learning curve for each and every one. We can learn to calculate the best way to deal with living through our handicaps, whether they be physical, emotional, psychological, or just plain difficult circumstances in life. Traumas, although at the time can be terrifying, can also bring out the best in us. They can give us the strength we need to combat any others that might come our way, thus making living each day a more realistic challenge.

As we develop, I think it would be correct to say, that we are each responsible for our own choices as to how we try to battle with problems and trials. Sometimes we can decide to focus on more positive thoughts, difficult as it might seem at the time. None of us escapes those feelings of despair and hopelessness on occasions, but having a different strategy to play can be beneficial, even though from my experience it takes practice and determination. I am encouraged by the words 'Rome wasn't built in a day'. It is said that strength and eventually beauty can come from struggles, as we begin to look differently at situations to get us through. As we start to focus off the problems to finer, more positive things, we learn to see something of value in hardship in whatever form. Looking for gold in tons of rock is hard work, as is finding a shaft of light in a dark tunnel, but the joy that can be felt when it happens must be unbelievable. Unfortunately, only by trying and working at this will we find out for ourselves. Perhaps as time teaches us to appreciate the many little sparkles of hope we find along the way, to encourage us to keep going, so eventually it will become second nature and we will move into a different realm. Gradually, as this process develops, I am sure changes within us will also start to happen. Confidence starts to grow and trusting in our own instincts could become a regular occurrence allowing us to take positive steps into the unknown.

Every opportunity that presents itself has the potential for seeking the best out of it at the time, even if it requires us to just look and see a little longer. What if each time our mood becomes despondent, depressed or irritated, we made a conscious decision to see the best in each situation we find ourselves in, when ordinarily we would just become more negative? Is it possible that by taking a few, simple, positive mind steps, our attitude and mood could be uplifted and our outlook become completely different? Perhaps, we might be able to train ourselves to eventually, consciously start looking for the possibilities of beauty and pleasure from difficulties and challenges we face. This might enable us to live in that particular situation with a lot less stress. I have to say that was a serious suggestion, and I am working on it to prove to myself that this is something that is inevitable, because negativity and positivity cannot exist side by side at the same time. This is a logical fact.

How much could we all gain in our lives if we mastered the art of eventually living almost each day relatively stress free, although it sounds too good to be true. High blood pressure would almost definitely become a problem of the past, not to mention the wrinkles on our faces which might well be less. Perhaps gradually becoming more like fine lines, without the aid of expensive night creams. Perhaps comfort eating would become null and void and sleepless nights just a memory. I cannot say that this is a cure for the above, but I do think that these issues could be more easily managed if we could learn to refocus on an alternative way of looking at problems and difficulties. Time might eventually show us the enjoyment we could gain from what otherwise could just remain as trauma. Awe and wonder does not run after you; you have to find it within your heart.

Why not try it for yourself? The next time you find yourself feeling empty, negative or downhearted, look around you with new eyes of interest in what you actually see. It is so easy not to see what we are looking at when our minds are focused and being driven by intense negative, tension provoking thoughts whether from within, which at the time we are probably not really aware of, or from without. By focusing on the different aspects of colour, texture, shapes and sounds around you, you might appreciate what you are seeing in a new way. These moments of seeing have to be actively sought to be experienced, they will always be there, but we can so often look straight through them with blind, unseeing eyes. Nothing about what you see is changed, but the way you see it has, which is where life could take on a very different meaning.

Why would we not want to find ways to create a more peaceful outcome to situations, which might otherwise be laden with anger, fear and rebellion? By effectively seeking out and pondering on the more positive influences, from many unpredictable situations, we can turn many negative emotions into positive ones. Once we consciously train our minds to think and see things differently, living and the way we experience it has to reach a different level. A level of being able to enjoy any number of circumstances which come our way in whatever form. Being willing to accept, that even if we can't change our situations, we are able to alter the way we react to them, especially in what we see, feel and fear. As we participate in our new-found experiences on a different level, our very existence will take on new meaning, and over time this will eventually start to become a natural occurrence, perhaps every day. It is never too late to refocus on other ways of reacting, to what life has to throw at us, but it takes determination and an open mind to change certain patterns of negative thinking and negative reactions which can be hard to break.

Chapter 9

Is it Time to Let Go?

Why are we so afraid to let go. Let go of anything, absolutely anything.? As you look around you, you might think that what you see are the things you need, but the question that springs to mind is, who says you need them and why? I would suggest we are products of our environment and conditioning, and if we were to question too deeply what we are comfortable with, we might find ourselves becoming uncomfortable.

Of course, we can temporarily live without many things for a short while, but we always know that more often than not, they can or will be replaced. However, letting go of material things, which we have known around us for some time we might find difficult to give up, because over time they have become so familiar to us. We hardly stop to think if we could really manage without them, until perhaps we are forced into a situation where we may have to consider it, especially if they have sentimental value. Something that has always puzzled me is that in one street of maybe 20 houses, if we went to do a house check, we would more than likely find, 20 lawn mowers, and garden tools, 20 – 30 cars, and 20 sets of garden furniture etc. etc. etc. and yet we could not in a million years imagine sharing these resources for long. Why not, what are we afraid of? I am not sure, but what I do know is that an accumulation of possessions is a means of security for many of us, and to imagine life without them could mean we might lose some of that security. Perhaps also materialism gives a sense of identity to those who are in need of it for whatever reason. Life without things, for some would have little or no meaning, sad but true. Replacing old for new seems to have become a disease, which has no cure, mindless spending day after day, week after week, is the result. In our consumer led society nothing much appears to please us more.

Sometimes I stop to think about the current refugee crises all around different parts of the world and if I am honest it is hard to empathize with those who have lost so much. We even see it with our own eyes on the TV etc. families torn apart, running for their lives with NOTHING, just a baby in arms or a carrier bag. For us in the West it is difficult to appreciate what those families are dealing with and the feelings they are having to endure. We have so much materially in every way, that we can hardly identify with their horrific circumstances. Is it any wonder that we are unable to feel much for their plight which hardly impacts us for long even when we do. The tragedy of those fleeing for their lives, having lost everything, cannot really impact us or really be understood. Having to let go of what was probably a frugal life style anyway, they have also now lost their dignity, self-respect and the country they more than likely grew up in most of their lives, and would have grown to love. Families torn apart, to having no future to dream about, only more loss, more pain and total uncertainty and loss of identity.

The two contrasts we are seeing have no connection, they are worlds apart, which is why we cannot even contemplate what is happening in the parts of the world which we cannot see. It is easier to harden our hearts, with little or no empathy, to the suffering of those out there whose situation changes nothing for us! Why should it? We have everything we need and more. Life goes on just the same and when some of those in such dire need, find themselves in our society in such extreme poverty, I have heard it said, "We can't take on any more struggles from oversees, they will deplete our resources and cause hardship to the society in which WE live!" Can it be that we as a nation have become so greedy, so selfish and so self-centered, we are incapable of reaching out without resentment to those human beings, who through no fault of their own have been left with nothing except the clothes they stand up in. They don't even have hope!! Fortunately, I think this attitude towards the needy is only amongst the minority. Letting go of just a little from every family in this nation could mean the world to so many of these misplaced persons, but more importantly, would allow them to feel that they were really worth giving to. That alone might contribute to helping restore their dignity and self- worth, enough to learn to live again.

Another form of letting go is about moving on from past hurts and troubles, bad memories from past relationships or resentment to name but a few. Rumi (a 13th Century Persian poet, theologian and Islamic scholar) wrote "The moment you accept what troubles you've been given, the door will open". The above differs a lot from materialism, as these tend to be involved with emotions as opposed to things. Even so I am sure, when considered with regard to letting go, it is probably based on similar feelings of insecurity. The emotional ties from the past can be like a warm blanket, when there is nothing or no one to replace them, and when we feel cold a warm blanket can be a great comfort to most of us. Thinking about tomorrow, when we don't have our warm blanket from the past wrapped around us, can be hard and for some impossible. It's as though we need a replacement before we can even think about letting go. In fact it could be said, some even need a substitute to fill the gap that would be left. Maybe that's why we hang on to old negative memories, which seem better with each passing day as we struggle to let go of them and move on. Past relationships seem better than they actually were as we fight to let go and be single again. It's as though everywhere we look there are couples around us enjoying a sublime partnership, which we have just lost, but that definitely may not be true. Perhaps hanging on to old relationships fills the gap of loneliness and despair we might feel if we were to move on into the unknown. Getting stuck in the past has no future, why not make peace with the past and move on. Living in the toxic territory of regret and negativity we are in danger of ending up in a place of losing.

However, once again, time is a great healer and letting go becomes easier as the days and weeks go by, and slowly but surely we can move on to find happiness again, perhaps from within ourselves where we can be sure it will stay. Loving ourselves is the only true place to move on from. Negative emotions only bring misery and suffering to ourselves in the long term and finding the strength to face reality about ourselves and our past failures is very necessary if we want to live a fulfilled and positive life. Happiness can only come from within us when we truly accept and love ourselves despite our failings and disappointments. Relying on happiness from outside ourselves is rarely ever permanent. On the contrary with inner happiness, no one or nothing can take that away from us, at least not for long. From that position we can hopefully find new beginnings for as much or as little as we choose to. Rumi believed, 'Life is a balance between holding on and letting go'.

Chapter 10

Is it time for change?

Have you ever imagined being stuck in a time zone, each day like the day before, or the future being just like the present? I guess we would have the knowledge in advance that we were never going to grow old, so would never need to consider our futures, because they basically wouldn't exist. Perhaps scientists may one day invent a pill that will help us to become ageless and we will never have to think about death as we know it. How in the world could we exist in such a way? I think it could so easily become boring beyond belief.

The Seasons would just disappear; therefore, nothing would have to be sown in order to reap. Nothing would die as such because ageing wouldn't happen. We would not need ambition because in time even that could become mundane and fruitless, even though healthy ambition is a power tool which encourages us to grow and develop our brain cells. Any eagerness to succeed would be null and void, eventually wasted as we discovered that we had no need of it. We would have no need to grow physically because in some science books growing is classified as ageing, and that wouldn't be necessary. I might suggest that we would probably be different from each other, but with no set purpose, life as we know it would not really exist. Without any need to grow up, our world would become smaller and our individual worlds would become suffocating. How could we exist in this way if everything remained the same? I actually believe that without change life could not exist, however basic or mundane it might become. Gail Sheeny (the author of Turning Chaos into Confidence) suggests "If we don't change, we don't grow. If we don't grow we are not really living".

In the same way that we cannot stop time ticking by, change is inevitable. No matter what we might want to think about it we cannot avoid it; in fact, we probably need to embrace it. Whether it is change taking place around us or from within us, needless to say it has to happen. Looking at the long term situation, it would appear change is for the better, even though sometimes many of us struggle with that belief. Looking at another perspective, many developing changes have brought less suffering in the world around us, including our own families. I am certain that many changes are unforeseeable at the time but none the less just as important. 150 years ago who could have imagined the mobile phone or the internet and how bizarre it is we are now so dependent on such things. Our lives are being controlled and dominated by these technical discoveries and inventions that we can hardly imagine life without them. Who would have thought a few years ago that developing pictures from our cameras would almost become extinct? No one knew at the time, what the outcome of the inventor's exploratory minds would be. The why, how and when questions had to be answered, as the more enquiring amongst them, never faltered in their keenness to understand and make sense of life. I am sure fear could have been the greater emotion on occasions, whilst searching for explanations, even though curiosity and tenacity eventually won the day.

Change brings its' own terrors to our sometimes habitual way of life, and to some extent, I think we are all keen to avoid the insecurities that might come our way because of it. One such issue the growing number of people living on our planet earth. Nations are now worried about global starvation, which are problems far removed from the time of the hunter-gatherer, when nothing could have been further from their imagination! Society is now in a place of wondering, which is more impossible to believe, our history or our future. Both have a part to play in our existence, but if you stand still long enough and think about it, you can find yourself wondering which is more inconceivable. Life has evolved to mean so many different things to the world in which we live, bringing unforeseen opportunities to many, although probably only taken up by a few. Who can say what great advances would have never been made for the future, if some great mistakes had not been made in the past. We owe it to ourselves and to those amazing people and happenings, to embrace the fulfilling moments that those changes have brought our way. All be it often with an unknown destiny, those changes have helped to put the beating pulse into life itself. Some of course might cringe at the risks involved in finding new pastures in which to pass their time, or new people to meet and get to know, but for some searching for new experiences in life can be exciting and interesting.

Our differences are what makes life challenging, but being resistant to change may need deeper consideration. We are here for such a short time compared to eternity, or our understanding of it. None of us are the same, which is why our perception of life can be so different. Even so, we cannot afford to be complacent about our existence as we each understand it to be. Because of change, life has evolved over time, to mean so many different things to the world in which we live. It can bring unforeseen opportunities that may never have come our way. Being willing to make changes can be frightening, but also exciting. No one knows what the outcome might be when they take a step into the unknown. Change can be breath taking, but also scary, and it is understandable that hesitation can be the greater emotion. Responsibilities can be an issue when wanting to experience change in our lives and for a given time can hinder our moving out of our comfort zone. However, they may not be forever around us and then, if our appetite is still hungry for the unknown we can manoeuvre our lives in order to make it happen. Manipulating our escape route can take years of planning or it can happen in a moment! The fact that we are willing to choose an alternative to the life we live is the first step, although some may never travel along such lines of thought. Whatever your experience it will be important to you, and each of us will eventually have the choice to move on or stay just where we are. Complexities of life can be restricting and could seem like too much trouble and effort to struggle with, in order to leave our everyday pattern of living, but those who want to engineer a way round them I am sure could find great reward. We will encounter many hurdles even in the thinking process, which could be overwhelming, but with a little extra determination and patience it could be possible to convert those thoughts into actions.

As time passes and we inevitably get older in years it is said that change becomes more difficult. I have to say that I don't totally agree with that philosophy. I think a more objective appraisal might be, that as we age we are perhaps more discerning about the changes we choose to accept, and are less fearful in saying no. When young there is a tendency to jump in at the deep end, so to speak, and maybe not consider if we are able to swim. before long there could be the possible doubts or regrets as time goes by. Fortunately, the passing of time allows each of us to find a balance in all things and I feel that this is definitely one of those times. Growing through time shapes our ability to look at all aspects of change, not only within ourselves, but also in society, whether it is at home, or in the world around us. Certainly, it has to be said that ageing is not all bad and can have great advantages as we grow in wisdom through experience. Miguel de Cervantes Saavedra wrote in Don Quixote "Time ripens all things. No man is born wise"

Chapter 11

A Time to be Free

Have you ever really considered in any depth the true meaning of being free? Oprah Winfrey (American television personality, actress, and entrepreneur) suggests being free is the right to choose. I suppose because we in this country live in such relative freedom, compared to so many in the rest of the world, we rarely consider what being free really means. I began thinking about the way we can walk out of our homes, travel in and out of cities and rarely think twice about why we shouldn't. We consider it nothing to sometimes travel around the country on our own, and even contemplate travelling abroad alone, as I have done more than once. Shopping is an everyday occurrence and our regular visits to coffee houses are a must. In fact, we cannot really imagine being unable to do such things. We are free to come and go as we please, nobody actually is that interested. Except, if we were to leave the country and endeavour to enter other new frontiers. I would say we take it pretty much for granted as it is all we have probably ever known.

Some however, are not born free, and it is not unheard of for men and women to have to account to others for their whereabouts, and to be questioned as to where they might want to go and why. Freedom of speech and action could be curtailed if it is thought that it might disrupt the status quo. Free expression or individuality might be seen as a risk or threat to those in authority, and we might well wonder why? It could be thought that behind these controls, there is a subversive action being played out, on a daily basis. The desire to suppress or oppress is so strong that you can't help but think that there must be some underlying issues at work. Is it human nature to use authority, with which inevitably comes power, to intimidate others in whatever way possible? Crushing anything that stands in its way, irrespective of cost, whether it be money, position or relationships. Freedom of choice could be seen as a hindrance to the success of the above, especially if it challenges the motivation behind the controls, and calls into question the necessity of the same for whatever reason. A seemingly innocent desire to make choices, could be interpreted as an expression of trying to hinder or confuse the controlling factors at work.

Interestingly, when you watch children at play, it is noticeable that one or other of them never ceases to try to be the boss or dictate how games or actions should be played. It seems to be human nature for someone to want to be in charge. My question is why? What is it within us that demands that position and if not given will take it anyway? We don't have to teach children to be this way, it seems to be ingrained in their personalities from the moment they start to walk or talk. My observation is that whilst watching any group of children at play, there are almost always the doers or the takers. Also, the passive and aggressive natures, but what develops the differences I wonder? I think we all have the capability, even as children to want to be the biggest or the best, and we don't care what it costs to get there. Perhaps it is based on ambition. Maybe, some are more driven to achieve and do their best than others, and if it means having to work harder or longer to succeed rather than lose, then maybe that is the driving force.

However, being free, it has to be said, is not necessarily just the desire of humans. Watching a caged animal is a sad and frustrating pastime. The inability to engage in activities such as hunting etc., renders it unable to enjoy the physical achievement and exercise that these activities would bring. They are instinctively always looking for ways to escape from rabbits to lions. At the first opportunity that presents itself most will run off determined to be free. On the other hand, it is a joy to watch beautifully coloured butterflies, enjoying the sunshine on their wings, as they dart freely from one flower to another. Why would anyone want to take away that pleasure by trapping them in a glass or plastic container? Have you ever watched free range chickens wandering here and there, completely oblivious to their surroundings, whilst pecking around looking for food all day long.? They never seem to stop, except when the sun goes down, when they willingly go back to the chicken house to spend the night sitting on a perch to sleep. I can't think of anything more uncomfortable but they love it. The misery of battery hens cannot be imagined when you have seen and enjoyed watching the complete opposite.

Most living and breathing creatures need to be free as do humans, but unfortunately it is well known from various sources such as television media, and books etc. that that is not the case. We still hear of those living in unenviable situations where respect of choice is not a priority. Freedom is just a meaningless word for so many, unable to experience its true meaning as we know and understand it. Even so in the midst of tragedy and afflictions, human beings have incredible tenacity and strength to find other ways to console themselves, as many war torn countries can testify. Perhaps, in some strange way, there is a certain freedom experienced in trying to learn how to survive and battle against forces beyond their control. The desire to survive becomes the most important, consuming objective, which at the same time overrules the long term joy of freedom, especially when it comes to avoiding destruction. Faith must have to be called upon from deep within the human soul, and some would say, the driving force which brings hope and endurance to those in the greatest of struggles; struggles which most of us who live in such privileged circumstances can never imagine.

What defines freedom as a concept to be lived each day? As I see it, it all boils down to one word and that is choice, without choice there is no freedom. Obviously and ultimately nature designs its' own natural order, and manmade social order tries to encourage and allow us to live peacefully and as harmoniously as possible, but even this requires choice. Of course, there will be consequences to bad choices if they incur pain or suffering to another's welfare, but I think most of us want to live contentedly with our friends and neighbours. Having freedom of choice can allow us to become the individuals we are born to be, with different skills and ambitions. It allows us to grow and develop our own personalities and characters every day, and who can say where it will lead us. It gives us the ability to teach others and to identify need in our brothers and sisters and I don't just mean siblings. We can choose to listen and learn, or turn a blind eye to the amazing freedom that comes with education. It brings knowledge and knowledge is power, which we can use to make our world a better place for all, irrespective of colour, age or environment. Perhaps there are those in our world, who feel threatened by being made aware of the freedom that can come from learning and education, so they treat it as a low priority. Even so, I believe mankind has a hunger and determination to learn and educate their minds against the most insurmountable odds.

Writers throughout history have succeeded in making unforgettable contributions to society, even though some were imprisoned, murdered, exiled or forgotten for trying to do so. Irrespective, their words have lived on, and have since been read and acted upon. The power to influence through words can also bring freedom of choice, by many being able to read and learn about the different cultures in our world. Different levels of understanding, created by the need to know, feeds the mind and allows an individual to discern between the different options and choices available. Time over the centuries has proved that education brings freedom of choice which otherwise would never be understood. Many injustices have been brought to light in this country, down through the ages, by literature exposing the truth. The detrimental living conditions, and lack of social and political concern to change anything during the Victorian era were regularly exposed by Charles Dickens. His exposure of such injustices, and poverty expressed through the freedom to write the truth, has brought changes which are indisputable and life changing.

The human race generally I am sure, lives in hope of a time coming soon, when all mankind will be enjoying their own time of freedom. It would be amazing to dare to believe, that as time goes by, the gap between those who don't live freely and those that do will be extinguished altogether, so that they could experience what is the right of all. We continue to live in hope that one day this might become a reality and that freedom of choice will not be only for the minority. Controlling any individual against their will, unless they are a threat to humanity, must be far beyond what most would consider normal or necessary. Individuality, developed in societies within the parameters of tolerance, security and understanding, must be the right of everyman or woman, thus giving all individuals the freedom of choice they have a right to and which they deserve.

Chapter 12

Stop this Train – I want to get Off!

Have you ever been travelling on a train, and suddenly realised that you were on the wrong one, and you were not going where you thought you were heading. It's inconceivable to think there is only one absent minded person around, who has found themselves in this unenviable position. In my experience, in a moment's notice you experience a feeling of slight panic washing over you, which is short lived, knowing you can get off at the next station. Then annoyance starts to emanate for not checking properly before alighting the said train, all-be-it probably through a lack of time, which really is no excuse. Then, the mounting realisation of all the inconvenience and time wasting which is about to ensue floods your mind, which unfortunately you have no option but to accept. Knowing there is no point stressing over what is now a thing of the past, if only by minutes in some cases, most of these feelings can be easily overcome.

It's true to say in most cases, before travelling any journey we firstly make a decision as to where we are going and secondly, how we are going to get there. We trust that we have made all the right choices in our planning, and that the journey will have very few problems or delays along the way. Of course it is certainly more than likely, if not inevitable, that however much research and planning we have done for our journey, it may not turn out the way we expect. We are unable to predict mishaps, and cannot be sure that there will be no breakdowns. It is only a matter of time before we realise we are actually at the mercy of many others as to how and where we might end up, and more importantly, when?

It recently occurred to me that life could be a bit like this scenario. Most people, travel along through life, being conditioned by our upbringing, social training, school education and interactions. In fact, it could be said we are products of our environments. However, as we grow older, we have a tendency to start to analyse our existence and way of life, and where we are going with it. Some could be forgiven for thinking, life is what it is; you are where you are, even though you are not completely sure how you got there. Looking back you can see that over time certain situations have developed, some of which you had an influence over and others, which appear on the surface to have just happened. Either way, you have arrived where you are now, and as such it is 'fate accompli.'

Is the journey of life really any different? We are on a path which we often think we have chosen, but on closer examination we find that maybe that isn't the case. Through different circumstances, we might have taken a route, which at the time was seemingly the only way to go. Perhaps through lack of time, or interest or knowledge, we travel our journey of life, which takes us to a different location from where we first anticipated. Is it possible, that we might have made a different decision, had we had more time to consider the long term consequences of our actions? However, once the decision has been taken, no matter how long ago, there is a sense of no turning back. Then there are sometimes outside influences, which can put us under pressure, to stay where we are and not to question our decisions. A fear of having possibly made a wrong decision in the past, may start to create anxiety and a feeling of tension which is difficult to shake off, especially if more than one person is involved in the outcome. Before long we could be struggling with doubts about where we are heading and why?

Unfortunately, at this point the circumstances we may now find ourselves in, may be very different as to when we started out on our journey. Commitments and responsibilities are now more evident, and fears of the unknown are causing a sense of panic. Change is always threatening, but especially when we are unsure of where we might be heading if we were to suddenly, unusually change course. During the passing of time, unpredictable influences may easily have come to bear on our original plans. Instead of any changes affecting just ourselves, there could be others whose considerations can't be ignored, possibly making the way forward awkward and stressful to pursue. This situation could cause some to think no change is better than the current situation, and they choose to carry on as before, only now pretending to themselves that it doesn't matter. Of course for some this may turn out to be the best solution I believe this is the point where we need to stop, to press the pause button and replay what has already happened and rethink the planned journey. A bit like replaying a part of a film we have missed. Perhaps pausing the film and pressing re-play will help to make sense of what we have been watching and thus the ongoing story later.

Of course for some this may turn out to be the best solution. However, some might prefer to deal with the situation another way. People are very different, and some might prefer to get off the train, and re-focus on where they are heading and why? Any growing uncertainty they might have been feeling could become worse if they were to bury it rather than question their decisions. For them, looking at the long term picture would definitely help to get things in perspective. The knowledge of ending up in the wrong place for the wrong reasons would be their motivation for changing course. Any sense of failure for them is better dealt with at the time, rather than in the future when circumstances might be more impossible to deal with. Any fear might need to be challenged, rather than hidden, and the possibility of honestly facing a change of direction is preferable. Making an opportunity to pause and replay could turn out better than ending up at the wrong location sooner or later. For many facing doubts and fears head on could be a lifesaver, rather than burying them in the hopes they will go away, or worse still ending up in a different location rather than the one that was once planned. Time given to re-evaluating would be time well spent to enjoy a more secure and thus enjoyable outcome.

It will probably require courage and a willingness to be criticised or questioned by those close to us who probably won't quite understand why it might be necessary to change direction. Pushing through these barriers and relocating has its' own price to pay, but what price might there be if we don't? I believe we only pass through this life once and we owe it to ourselves to be able to admit that maybe the choices we made were not as ideal as we had once thought or planned. To exercise the courage to face the challenge of stopping the train and climbing off, when it has been made clear to us that we are not going in the right direction, could turn out to be costly. It doesn't necessarily mean costly as in financially, but of course that might have to be considered. No, I mean costly as in being willing to admit that we might have chosen wrongly and therefore need to pay attention to the fact. Keeping an open mind and being willing to spend time to rethink our once chosen path, might be necessary, without being rushed or influenced by others.

There is a school of thought that would suggest that those who hesitate are lost. Let's just say everything in moderation might be the key to keeping the balance now and in the future.

Chapter 13

The Ravages of Time

The dictionary describes perpetual motion as constantly moving, never stopping or being still. As you can imagine, constant movement must require an immense amount of energy to sustain itself, which means a lot of energy is not available for anything else. I suppose you could liken it to a clock ticking or a tap dripping, until it breaks down it will not stop. I think it is possible that we humans could also find ourselves in perpetual motion, engaging in endless activities to fill any spare time we might have, almost afraid to stop. Why do some of us have an insatiable desire to keep our bodies or minds constantly moving, so any thoughts of being able to do nothing or very little, elude us? Why is inactivity so difficult to accept in our daily lives, that even striving for what can sometimes be unachievable goals, can be more attractive and easier to accommodate? Is it possible that we do not want to make our lives simpler, because we are not sure what we could possibly achieve by sitting or standing still? Perhaps we do not trust where our inactivity might lead us. As we contemplate our future, maybe all we can see is continuous activity, in order to achieve our wants and desires. The problem is how do we measure our success and by what? The only measure I can think of is the expectation that others have placed on us, in the past or now.

Is it possible that the fear of failure is a driving force constantly snapping at our heels? We may or may not be aware of this because it is possibly so deep rooted. Maybe if we never finish what we have started, we will never find out if we might have failed or not, we can just carry on regardless. Another reason might be, by never saying no to anything or anyone can keep us in submission of our need to be accepted. Is it possible we really do not believe or accept we are good enough, in which case we can never stop trying to please others? Receiving constant admiration helps to boost our self-esteem. I suppose it would be easy to spend time blaming our past situations for the reasons why we have been unable to stop and slow down. Will there ever be a point where we can learn to accept ourselves for who we are and what we stand for? Is it possible, as we each mature in age, we might be more willing to look at ourselves and appreciate what we are becoming, or what we have become?

I believe each human being has a purpose in this life, and although our conditioning, through upbringing and socialisation may knock us off course for a while, everyone can go back and do a rethink. Recognising there are endless opportunities for re-evaluation, if we so wish, we can search with renewed enthusiasm for new possibilities. It merely requires energy, and honesty, and a desire to spend time reflecting on where we are and where we could be. For some, considering they might have made some wrong choices could be almost impossible to think. Deciding on a new direction, which may also not turn out right, requires a lot of thinking about, so sometimes it is easier to ignore such thoughts. By keeping ourselves busy, so there will be little time to think about such things, is a great way to avoid any changes or adjustments that might be useful.

The ravages of time can also affect our bodies, and the effects are undeniable, as they can be easily apparent. They say we start physically deteriorating as soon as women reach approximately 25 years old and men reach 23, but we tend to try to forget such information exists. It would be reasonable to think, 'What is the use in knowing such things when we are unable to do a thing about it?' Up to a point that is true, but on the other hand pausing for thought is not such a bad thing. For example constantly doing something physically demanding could result in causing us physical pain or deterioration By being sensible and searching out another form of physical exercise, which might be less stressful on our wellbeing, would definitely be advantageous. Striving for perfection, in whatever form, is time consuming and probably exhausting. The level of perfection that we might not consider acceptable to ourselves could be perfectly acceptable to others. I suppose, at the end of the day, it all comes down to our knowing what level of satisfaction we are happy to accept, and our willingness to draw a line under it. Ultimately, this might require us to stop and resist our labour intensive lifestyles.

As I see it, the only person we have to live with is ourselves, and what we can accept about how we do that is up to us. Taking time out to evaluate what we are doing and why, can be easier said than done for many of us, especially when we are all able to make excuses for why we are too busy. Allowing everything around us to dominate our decisions, rather than slow down and exercise choice, is probably the easier path to choose for many. The fact of the matter is asking ourselves these type of questions, which may be difficult to answer, requires courage and a willingness to accept the truth about what we might discover. Perhaps having to rethink about the situation, we find ourselves in for some might be easier. I guess that is up to each individual who dares to search deeper than the surface, unfortunately, no one else can do it for us.

Chapter 14

Thinking Time

Do you have time to think? It really does not matter much about what, but more importantly, do you have time? Put another way do you put time aside to consider what has happened yesterday or today and why? Did I plan it, was it fate, or was it just a passing of time, of no interest to anyone? Some say it is futile to think about the past, and others might think, 'why waste time thinking?' There will always be the usual questions such as, why are we here? What is the point of life? What is it all about? These questions are not for this time and place because each has its own individual outcome and destiny. Many believe that every action starts with a thought and every action creates a reaction. It would seem that the process of thinking could be responsible for many things besides just being a thought.

The what-if thoughts spring to mind the typical curiosity questions, which bring otherwise dull situations to life, very often with a funny outcome. However, it is possible, these curiosity questions can sometimes be responsible for challenging and dynamic changes, which at the time, could not have been imagined? Inventors and scientists are not afraid to act on what if questions, in fact, I am sure they must find them quite exciting to pursue, and have led to many new additions to technology in the past and certainly for the future. Just a simple enquiring thought which little by little has led to actions far beyond our understanding. Many of us might find this uninteresting, but we definitely owe our progress since time began to those kind of folk. Scholars have spent forever thinking over questions, which perhaps never realised an answer, but none the less are important to many, just in case they do. I can imagine we shall always share our lives with challenges, which require a lot of energy to be spent on silent thought, whether we find an answer, or if the answer we find is to our liking is another matter altogether. Time is costly, and we lead such busy lives, that some might consider spending time in a thinking mode ill spent. There are so many things to do, places to go and people to see, that it is more likely to be at the bottom of the list of things to do. Not a priority so to speak in the wider scheme of living.

Another aspect of thinking is that it sometimes requires us to spend time alone. Being alone with our thoughts is not to each of our likings, most certainly not for very long anyway, probably reminding us of feelings of isolation. Some of us struggle with the idea of spending time alone with our thoughts because it could become anxiety provoking, so it is easier not to think too much. Using isolation as a punishment, in many forms and places in the past and more than likely in the present also, for various different reasons. Being away from others could feel like a form of deprivation, which can make some individuals feel quite vulnerable. Being alone is not for humans they say, and sharing ones' life and thoughts and feelings is a natural need in most of us. Even so, perhaps the best thinking time is done, when given solely to it, even if it is only for a short while. Making thinking time available in-between everyday demands, can be an essential way to maintaining a balance, between being crazy with stress or being able to stay calm and focused.

Sometimes, the question of having to cope with unwelcome thoughts may be something that needs to addressed, but busyness can easily hide the desire to put this into action. How much easier it is to hide behind busyness instead of dealing with issues which require honesty and reflection. Time is never easily available for such things, so not making space for them is easier than confronting them. We convince ourselves, that everything is more important than dealing with issues, which may have been outstanding for a long time. Burying them, by not allowing ourselves to give them the thinking time they need, unfortunately does not make them go away. Time is a great healer but I am sure, it will not be as effective as it could be, if not given the respect that belongs to it. However, although running away can seem easier on occasions, it does not always allow progress. I think we would all enjoy a life, that is exciting and non-confrontational, but how realistic is that when human beings are involved? Spending a little time reflecting on past or current difficult moments can make or break relationships, especially when time given to building up, rather than tearing down can be the cement that has needed to sustain even the most difficult shaky foundations. Surely, anything worth keeping is worth spending time on, especially relationships, in order to protect them from the daily bitter elements that can come against them. Daily misunderstandings often require compromise, which is difficult to accomplish without the sharing of thoughts.

Of course, there are those who think that life is too short to waste time thinking, and I suppose it depends a great deal on each person's evaluation of what wasting time means. One person's interpretation of time wasting is not necessarily the same as another's. This must be a good thing, because it means, we each have a certain independent outlook on life and therefore our thoughts are different. It is arguable that time is passing us by when we spend a lot of time thinking, and before we know it is gone and the next day, week, month or year takes over. Perhaps this could be 'Food for thought'.

Chapter 15

Is it Time to Forgive and Forget?

The question is, is it possible? This is a difficult question to answer and much depends on your own experiences as to how you might want to answer it. To be honest, I am not sure that it would be appropriate for everyone to share how he or she might feel about forgiving and forgetting, unless of course wishing to do so. Even so, it is a common thought and understanding, that sharing one's feelings can be helpful on many occasions, although it is also widely understood that the circumstances are what make the difference.

When hurting no one can hurt as you do, and we all have a tendency to think and feel that no one has ever experienced pain like ours. We can only exist at the time in a vacuum, which seems and feels like it will never end. Unfortunately, when in the situation, it is difficult to look outside of ourselves to see what other people see. It also matters how much hurt and pain or injury happens, at the time or in the past, whether it is physical or emotional. Knowing that almost no one can get through this life without having to forgive someone at least once, somehow gives us the ability to cope, as many in the past have done. Even though, there are many books written about every aspect of the consequences of un-forgiveness, it is a very different matter, when we are struggling in the situation, and it seems we just cannot take that step, or in some cases even think about it.

Talking from experience of many situations of a similar nature, I know that I struggled for years to understand what forgiving really meant. Only when you have been deeply hurt do you have to think about it or not as the case may be. Firstly, for me there is a need to understand why it had to happen at all. I could not go a step forward into forgiving until I had spent time trying to put things in perspective. It was a bit like expecting me to be able to find my way to somewhere without a map. Forgiveness was not a known entity, and I needed a token of information about my journey, to get there. Some might differ in their approach to forgiveness, and I expect it depends a lot on their purpose for considering doing it in the first place, but for me it just made sense. I suspect that holding on to un-forgiveness, could feed any revengeful feelings we might be experiencing at the time, although I am not sure we would be able, or want to admit that to ourselves. Revenge at the time might be the only emotion that we are able to feel, when the pain we are suffering is from the hand of another. Somehow, hanging on to it helps us to justify our anger. Carrying on judging another's hostility or bad behaviour towards us, can be another reason to continue living in the pain we have suffered or are suffering. Endless hours of engaging in repetitive thoughts, about how and why, can occupy our minds at the end of which we are sometimes none the wiser. Perhaps it helps to accept what has happened after the event, but I am sure that is a very personal thing for each one. This is easier to say than do for many, and the fact that it is often said with very little idea of the circumstances for those involved, it is probably no wonder it does not happen more often. Forgiving is one thing and forgetting is another. I personally am of the mind, that even if a person can find forgiveness in their hearts, they could perhaps find it impossible to forget. Fortunately, we are told that time is a great healer, and probably as such is the only way that forgetting is made more possible. We all have very different levels of sensitivity, which is what makes us who we are, and for some, a raw memory takes a long time to heal. Having spent some time thinking about this I am convinced that when we are ready and able to forgive, we will find the way to do it, even though it may end up costing us more than we thought, we were able to give.

The impact of any injustice towards oneself or another is difficult to ascertain for others, especially when the real facts about the issue are unknown, but the big question is, do we hang on to the hurt. There are many teachings on this subject, especially in religious realms, and for some it is expected forgiveness is a condition of living a full and righteous life. It is said that unforgiveness is a heavy burden that we carry, only at the expense of ourselves as it festers, and bitterness is its' replacement. It is hard to judge how this affects an individual, who may not be in the place they are required to be, in order to see things differently and take that step.

The Buddha teaches, "Holding on to anger is like grasping a hot coal with the intent of throwing it at someone else, but you are the only one who gets hurts". Wise words indeed. My view is that life is too short to be putting time into repeatedly going over the same bad thoughts or angry memories, and to continue to feel unjustly treated. The only way I have found to rid myself of the above has been to forgive the perpetrator and move on. I cannot testify to ever being able to forget the memories totally, although perhaps there must be some who have been able to do this. Although, the memories seemed so much more manageable and less upsetting to recall, having faded with the passing of time. Carrying a heavy bundle of negative emotions around with me was not that beneficial, and quite honestly could eventually end up making me feel a lot older than I wanted to feel. I eventually concluded that the extra weight was doing nothing for my muscle building and just really tired me out after a while.

Somehow, once forgiveness is given you feel so much lighter and able to focus on real positive thoughts, which enable you to look into the future with new eyes. Life is much more pleasurable when there are no dark places in which to hang around reliving our anger and resentment. Revenge to my mind is not actually sweet; it just makes our lives so much harder to live peacefully within ourselves.

Chapter 16

Is it Time to Forgive Yourself?

Forgiveness is not necessarily only about everyone or everything outside of ourselves; it is also good to understand the need to forgive us. Maybe we think it strange to forgive ourselves. I suggest there could be many reasons for this, but one reason which springs to mind, is that perhaps we don't feel we are worthy of forgiveness. Have you ever been in a situation where you knew this needed to happen but found it difficult to think about? I have a feeling most individuals find it is one of the most difficult things to do. Somehow being hard on ourselves, invites us to live with any guilt we may feel, because subconsciously this may feel like a form of punishment. Perhaps to judge ourselves is easier to live with, than the feelings of guilt we have become familiar with over time. Obviously, this is a very personal experience but for most of us, I believe it is necessary to live through mistakes, and accept they can happen to all of us at some time or another, before we can move forward. Hanging on to bad feelings such as negative thoughts about ourselves does not bode well for our health, and perhaps giving time to reasoning out our mistakes is a valuable thing to do. Looking into how we might avoid similar situations in the future, might be time well spent and talking about such things, is probably a good way forward if we feel able to do that. Many times sitting alone with negative thoughts does not have the desired effect to help us to see things in perspective.

Wishing past situations had never happened to my mind is not a fruitful pastime. Better to be honest and think, you cannot put the clock back and what has happened in the past is irreversible. However, in remembering our faults and misgivings, we can realistically focus on how we might avoid a similar situation occurring in the future.

Living with un-forgiveness from within ourselves is not easy and is not a happy position to live in. I am certain it is not something that anyone would choose for him or herself, and over the long term could be detrimental to relationships, in the future and to our health. Keeping guilt as a negative emotion in perspective, is an important part of the healing process, and needs to be realistically analysed. Overbearing punishments whilst growing up could be adding to our sense of unworthiness and inability to accept our own forgiveness. Long term feelings of disapproval from those in authority, can bear down on us and make us feel wounded beyond what we can understand at the time, and can leave us overreacting to mistakes we make as adults. Getting help to focus on what could be happening to cause this might be necessary, in order to get the peace of mind that we deserve, once able to admit our wrongdoing. Perhaps it has never crossed our minds that we can forgive ourselves, let alone why we should. Suffice to say that we cannot resurrect the past and nor should we.

Life carries on regardless. How much we can live with the past, will not only reflect on how we interpret the present, but also how we might look to the future. Being unable to find peace in our own hearts is a burden we will find heavy to carry around if there is no escape. Living everyday will be hard work, especially when we also have to give time and energy to just being able to cope with what life has to offer. Feeling unworthy can create a minefield of problems within ourselves, and we will not be able to see clearly, as to where we are going in the future. The only person affected by negative feelings of un-forgiveness will be the person who carries around such isolating feelings. Far preferable for us to remember, there can always be peace after a storm, however long it might take to arrive; we just have to embrace it with an open heart when it happens.

Chapter 17

A Time to Laugh

I have heard it said that laughter is the best medicine. I have also read a sense of humour could have a positive effect on our physical bodies, by causing us to relax, and therefore could help to keep our blood pressure balanced. In which case, I would like to dare to suggest, it might help us to live longer! I am not sure of the answer to that question, but I do know it makes you feel good. Everything else we hear or see on the media has the feel good factor at the top of the list, but inevitably, it is going to need us to dig deep into our piggy banks to pay for them. Just about, everything advertised will end up costing money, but not laughter. Up to this moment in time, it is absolutely, categorically without question free! There is not a manufacturer in the world that has managed to produce it and sell it on the open market, yet! Amazing is it not?

Laughter is definitely contagious, and I am sure we can all remember how when one person started to laugh, we so often found ourselves laughing alongside. Somehow, it was easy and pleasant to join in, even though on occasions, we really did not understand why. Joke telling was never one of my best attributes, because I always managed to forget the punch line, but it was easy to laugh at other's jokes. Spending time reminiscing about the past often brings heaps of laughter, and they are moments that hopefully we will never forget. We can find ourselves replaying them like an old record and each time they are just as funny. They never seem to lose their ability to amuse us repeatedly, especially when it involves remembering our childhood memories. I am sure there are many folks who have enjoyed such times whilst enjoying a pleasant evening with family and friends. Many of my fondest, funniest memories have been when my adult children have reminded me of the misdemeanours they got up to, some of which I knew about and some I didn't!!

Can you imagine a world without laughter? It is unthinkable and yet there are times when laughter, although free does not come easily to us, as much as we would like it to. Circumstances can sometimes dictate it is the farthest thing from our thoughts and we struggle to raise a smile let alone laughter. Life can throw many unpredictable happenings in our path, some of which can cause great sadness and trauma. Then even smiling can require a lot more effort, but I am sure that without it the world would be in a sorry state. Time however, is a great healer and before long, we can raise a smile, and soon laughter will be our friend again. Somehow, it rebuilds and gives us the strength to try again. Relationships, enriched by a mutual bonding through laughter, can empower us in times of need. Laughter helps us to demolish the walls of defence we think we need to protect ourselves, as we learn to trust again. It can break down barriers, class distinctions and unnecessary prejudices.

Then of course we can laugh at ourselves, sometimes harder to do, although if we are honest softens us. It helps us to realise that we really are only human, and humans can make mistakes, but it is ok. Eventually we can usually see the funny side of most situations, and that in turn lightens our load bringing relief, like taking off a heavy backpack. Perhaps laughter is not as easily acquired, or given time to, as we gather responsibilities in life. Yet it is none-the-less just as precious as it always was, still is, and will be in the future. Sometimes children can remind us of the joy of life and how simple it can be, by their innocent expressions of laughter. I know for myself, time spent with young children has a habit of leaving me feeling able to see the lighter side of life, bringing a sense of gratitude to my spirit. I am certain that we as adults could probably benefit from a healthy dose of this amazing medicine, to help keep us young, and to help us take life less seriously and more appreciatively

I think tough times, inevitable as they are, become easier with laughter on board. Why not take that special time out to de-stress and enjoy the simpler side of life, life which does not make its' own demands, but hastens to help you to be yourself and enjoy every moment. Crazy moments which will be imprinted on your memory for ever, and then when you have more time, in later years will come flooding back to you. Just so, you can relive your funniest moments and perhaps bring joy to others who may be struggling to find a smile. Believe me; I am certain they will be forever grateful. What they thought was then an insurmountable mountain could become a small hill to climb. Seeing the funny side of life is somehow more achievable when with a group of friends or family. Evenings spent looking at photos from the past, can trigger many funny, happy memories, maybe buried for many years in the filing cabinets of our minds, just waiting to be acknowledged once again only now, they can be an inspiration to many.

Laughter brings joy where there may once have been sadness, inspiration when it is hard to find, peace where there may have been turmoil and is a great antidote to stress. When all things are considered, perhaps laughter really could be the best medicine. Perhaps we should all make it our business to take a tablespoonful two or three time a day. Lets' face it, in this instance, prevention is definitely better than cure, would you not say?

Chapter 18

Is it time to stop wanting?

'The more you have the more you want', was one of my grandmother's frequent phrases, used as I was growing up. It did not mean too much to me then, but as I have grown older it has become more obvious what she meant, and what it probably still means today. As life is happening around me, it is easier to appreciate that what she said then, was probably right. It is interesting to contemplate her words and to evaluate the wisdom behind them. I suggest what the phrase was actually trying to express was human nature being what it is, there is a danger we may never be happy with what we have, because we will more than likely always want more! However, we can want forever and may never be satisfied, but surely somehow, there has to be a way to find a balance. As time passes, we may recognise, that certain things in life do not actually make us happy for long. There must be so many reasons as to why this could be the case. Even so, I am sure if left to consider this statement, you could come up with your own reasons or experiences familiar to yourself.

There has to be a way to make sense of this. Why, when we have enough, do we still want more? This has really puzzled me for a long time. It is almost like a disease that takes hold of us and it seems nothing can stop it. I prefer to believe we are not all greedy by nature even though the desire to accumulate seems insatiable. So are we just a consumer led society, constantly needing things to make us happy, as some would have us believe? Most certainly, if we were to take the TV commercials seriously, we shouldn't resist any of their hard selling, because their materials are essential to our existence. As I see it needing and wanting have become inseparable, in fact we could say they have eventually become one of the same. They used to be worlds apart in their meaning throughout history, but not anymore. The only problem is that because we want more, we have to earn more, to get more of things we want. Therein lays a tale. As we spend, so we must replace what we have spent, and before long, there is a situation where we find ourselves more and more needing to work harder, to provide for the hole in the bank balance. None-the -less for some, nothing seems to satisfy like spending money, even sometimes when we do not have it to spend.

Maybe it's possible, we are trying to fill any empty space within us, that doesn't seem to find satisfaction in any other way other than in accumulating 'things'. It is difficult to understand, but we are definitely not alone, as I am certain many share these feelings. However, being constantly hungry for more does not give us much time to enjoy what we already have, and therefore the need to feel satisfied is a long time coming. Would it be fair to say that perhaps wanting could be an expression of those unmet needs? Of course, I cannot be certain about this, but what I do know is that we humans will find a way to get what we want, perhaps blindly, in order to meet our needs and desires, even though the object of our desires may turn out to be not so good for us in the long term. Whether we want to emulate film stars, models, or pop idols, impress our friends or neighbours by what we have or how we look, or wanting a bigger car or house, only time will decide if these sought after objects are as fulfilling as we believe, or the media tell us they will be. It's possible we believe, or are led to believe, what we see outside of ourselves is the reality we should be aiming for, rather than the true reality of our own consciousness. Perhaps by looking inside ourselves, rather than at those around us, we will find answers that are more credible.

The problem is how does the deficit of any unmet needs get resolved? I am willing to suppose that may be they never do, or if they do, it is not so obvious at the time. Perhaps, the longing for things is never satisfied, because material things can satisfy us only briefly. The empty void remains because the novelty wears off or something new comes on to horizon. There will always be something newer, better, more efficient, faster and crazier than what we already have and they will leave us convincing ourselves that life is going to be so much better if we could just have them in our possession.

Research suggests we have a tendency to become products of our environment, rightly or wrongly, good or bad, and during this time, we learn to adapt and survive. Whether our basic needs are met, is almost the luck of the draw, so to speak. I wonder how many of us do just survive, whilst growing from baby to child and from child to adult, whilst having to adjust to changes and demands as part of our everyday learning experience. Eventually, it is possible we adapt our emotions to enable us to get the best out of our lives, but whether we develop, self-acceptance is another matter. To suggest that human beings are wanting because of being needy, could seem a bit far-fetched. However, it could be a possibility, and therefore we cannot afford to rule it out of the equation. The passing of time I am sure, will throw more light on the research being done, which in turn will help us all to become more aware.

Chapter 19

Do you have time to listen?

"Do you have time to listen?" "Listen to what?" You might well ask. I don't know if you have noticed, but we seem to live in a constant stream of noise. There is so much all around us and we are forced to listen to it. Consider this, virtually no shops don't have music playing constantly, from early morning till late at night. Almost every café, restaurant, or bar has the same. What ever happened to silence? "How can you listen to silence?" You ask. Well, I would suggest that the answer to that question might be, "Try it for yourselves". You might be surprised at what you hear. It sounds so crazy, but believe me it is possible. There is an expression used in our society that says 'I can't hear myself think'. I have often wondered what that phrase meant, but until I found a place where I could listen to silence, only then could I understand. It's an extraordinary thought, but I actually think it was more about allowing the silence to find me!

It is so easy to trundle along, being consumed by noises from every direction, they are almost drowning you! Distraction is the name of the game, there are uninterrupted, differing levels of voices all around. People having personal in-depth conversations on their mobile phones in public places, which you cannot ignore, totally oblivious that they may have a reluctant audience who would so much rather be somewhere else. Trains and buses spring to mind. Coffee shops are notorious, they draw us in to experience the beautiful aroma of coffee beans from distant lands, with flavours and strengths galore, but don't think for one moment this is the place to unwind and relax for long. There is no end to the grinding, swishing, steaming and constant clanging of cutlery and china! Somehow, we learn how to drown out the noise, otherwise we wouldn't do it. Perhaps, we really can't resist the temporary escapism that we enjoy, as we are transported to destinations far beyond our reach. After all we can all dream, all be it wide awake.

Why are we so accepting of this constant background noise? Maybe, we have no choice but to accept it, because most of the time everyone else does, and to complain we would definitely be in the minority. Perhaps on the other hand, it's easier in this noisy environment, not to listen to our own thoughts. Thoughts which we would rather evade, or bury, for fear of them making us feel awkward or uncomfortable. Perhaps we want to run away from issues which demand our concentration and honesty. Needless-to-say we must all have our own personal reasons for liking background noise. Being left alone with our own thoughts, can be awesome, for whatever reason, but can also be inspiring. To be able to concentrate on our thoughts for more than just a few minutes, could be so far removed from our everyday routine, it might take a little time to gradually acquaint ourselves with the experience. Spending time with our own thoughts, may even require us to plan ahead, in order to be physically alone. Listening to that still small voice within us, may not be easily recognisable at first, but gradually it will become familiar.

Listening to each other's needs, and situations can be demanding too, but I am sure is well worth the effort and time spent. Friendships are designed to encourage such things, but it is easy to make excuses to avoid such times. On the other hand, the receiver of your time, and the opportunity you give them to share their needs, will I am certain be eternally grateful. I am sure we cannot underestimate this truth. It is said that a problem shared is a problem halved. Putting time aside to listen to each other, to our children and our friends can also bring its' own blessings to each and every one of us. Also, if we were to consider how much pleasure we could get from listening to children's laughter and the joy it can bring to many of us, I am sure we would make sure we did it more often.

Making time to listen can come in all shapes and sizes, from people to nature, but for many reasons it is not always readily available. There are places to go, people to see and mountains to climb, on our busy daily schedules. At that moment nothing seems more important than getting the job done, but wait, let's take a rain check, is this really so? Are we really so very busy that we cannot spend just a little extra time with someone who would so appreciate it, but is too proud to ask. This precious time would be well spent and would bring its' own reward when least expected. Who can say what tomorrow may bring. Maybe one day we could be in a similar situation, and be so blessed by a few minutes shared with another. Do we really not have time to listen or put more directly, can we afford not to?

One of my most vivid memories is one of waving goodbye to an elderly person who lived alone, who saw no-one all day except the milkman or the postman. A daily carer spent 30 minutes with him and that was it!! Housebound and unable to meet anyone except these few folk, was all he had to look forward to, in the way of visitors every 24 hours. His only son lived miles away. His loneliness was unbearable, the television was his best friend, and if that failed the telephone might possibly take its' place. Perhaps someone to visit just to listen would have been so agreeable, but time is at a premium for most. I was left thinking, 'I hope that is never going to happen to me', which was such a selfish thought, but so true! None of us will escape the inevitable ageing process, but hopefully most of us will avoid the loneliness that could accompany it. Maybe on reflection we have to find the time to listen to others, because if we don't, time may never be found to listen to us in the future.

Chapter 20

Time for Making Memories

Why would we want to make time for making memories? Everyone I am sure will have his or her own thoughts about it, but from my own experience, I can see how very important it is. Enjoying what we have and even enjoying life, even though we do not have is how we create memories. It is not until later that we begin to realise that making memories is essential to our existence. Whether it is losing our ability to move fast, remember things, or just a sudden change in our circumstances for whatever reason, we can find ourselves looking back on our experiences and what they have meant to us. Little things, which at the time may have never been put into the calculation of making memories, suddenly light up, bringing untold pleasure when remembered, never-to-be forgotten. Of course, there are not so happy memories, which I am sure also, make themselves known, but it seems human nature has a tendency to remember more about happy times. Perhaps that is just as well, because it would be a very sad situation if all we had to live for, was to be constantly reminded how bad things were. Somehow remembering the good times seems to be easier and much more entertaining.

Children in particular, are amazing at remembering the good times, as opposed to the bad. Maybe it is nature's way of being sure of perpetuating the species, or maybe it is just life's way of protecting their sensitive fragile minds, even so, it is good to know. Perhaps it could also be a lesson to adults to be a little like children in our willingness to accept the good times and the bad, this way it is difficult to harbour resentment or bitterness. Making fond memories for a rainy day, might be more difficult by negative thoughts and feelings, as they definitely have a profound effect on our ability to remember well. Perhaps, remembering bad times, in some way helps us to feel better about our involvement in them. Most of us have the ability to blame shift, because it makes us feel so much better, even though we can possibly see faults may lie at our own door.

I think the mind wants to protect each of us, especially children, to block out hurtful and sad memories and why not? Clinging to negativity never did anyone any useful service, and certainly, builds a dam of resentment and grudges for later. Why torture ourselves with those things in the past, that seem to want to have no useful purpose, other than to more than likely make us feel bitter? Time passes by only once, relaying bad memories repeatedly can affect our perception of the future, which in turn has a way of creating an imbalance of expectation. Always walking in fear of what might happen can easily spoil what could. Taking a positive action in our thinking at the time of any unpleasant experience, negates the necessity to dwell on it, thus not encouraging a root of bitterness to take hold. Living comes with its own everyday challenges, without being loaded up with unwelcome negative influences, creating a haze of uncertainty in which to develop. Memories to some extent are stored away with permission and it is personal choice what we choose to do with them, how they affect our present and future, is pretty much up to each individual. We can choose to participate in storing bad memories in the archives of our minds to resurrect when we decide, or we can give them permission to float around in our minds in perpetual motion, creating disturbances. In turn, they can eat away at any positive or challenging experience, causing us not to enjoy a realistic and natural response to life. Constant bombardment from unpleasant, un-joyous memories can only surface when allowed, so long as we make sure they are stored away safely. Time itself will soon help us to forget where to find them, and as we concentrate on making new happy memories, will soon be forgotten. The only important factor here is that we try to make time for such in our busy lives.

It is easy to forget about putting time aside for creating and enjoying the more meaningful moments in our everyday lives, but as we spend time, doing this it will stand us in good stead forever, no matter how old we are. Also by spending time with our loved ones, we create moments when we can look back to remember the many happy occasions, which will never be lost. Filed away in the precious drawers of our hearts and minds, we cannot help but remember them with great fondness, especially when times get hard and life seems difficult to cope with. Each special memory wrapped up just like the old-fashioned love letters, hidden away to cherish and opened, when requested, as time allows. They play such an important part in our lives, even though we may not see it at that moment, and an even greater influence upon the future we may be about to create for ourselves. Clay Kaznarek 1982 – 2012 said, "What is Man but the sum of his Memories - we are the stories we live, the tales we tell ourselves" (Member of the Assassins Order).

Timeless and ageless, I am sure they could become a redeeming feature when the pace of life slows down. Many spend endless hours alone with their thoughts and cherished memories. When life is too demanding to do anything but watch and listen, due to illness or just the inevitable aging process, most of us will have to face many hours alone I am sure. Challenging as that might be, knowing we can reach into a wonderful array of specially stored memories, must I imagine, be a comfort and pleasure in years to come. It seems with aging comes the ability to remember from back in the past, so nothing would be wasted or forgotten. I do not know for sure because I am not there yet, but if and when the time comes, I hope I will have endless moments of recapturing the joyful memories stored neatly away for just such occasions. It will be a bit like making and then watching my own home produced vintage films, I being my own private audience. They will definitely never go out of fashion, nor will they cost me anything to watch but my time, which by then I will probably have more than plenty of!

Chapter 21

A Stitch in Time Saves Nine

Where ever did this old saying come from? I heard this phrase many times whilst I was growing up. I thought then, that it meant if you did not sew a tear up then it would get bigger and bigger, causing you more work in the end! I imagine, in the days when sewing machines were unheard of or very rare, everything was stitched by hand which must have taken forever. Gone are those days, but I think the saying goes on perhaps now, with a slightly different meaning? I understand now after doing some research it was an 'idiom', which is a phrase, which has a symbolic or intended meaning, which is different from the literal meaning of the words themselves. According to historians, it appeared in print in 1732 in Thomas Fuller's book 'Words and Quaint Counsels'. He was an English churchman and historian in London (1608 – 1661). Apparently its' meaning was quite simple. Do not procrastinate i.e. do not put off doing something until a later time, as it can probably create more work in the end.

This phrase could be applicable to every aspect of life if you stop and think about it for a while. Consider our health for example; the majority of young babies are born into this life as perfect, which is very different from 150 years ago. That very amazing little creature, that demands our attention from day one, is nothing more than a miracle. As the years go by and eventually independence comes to each one, there can be a misunderstanding about what is going to continue to keep that life as near as possible, to the perfection that baby was born with. Peer group pressure, media pressure and just sheer curiosity, are going to challenge that expectation all be it in varying degrees. Life expectancy has become longer and longer, and we could probably be excused from thinking, that it will never happen to me anyway! That could well be true, but in order to help that along, being attentive to what we put into our bodies should truly help. Warnings about many issues to be wary of are worth remembering, if we would want to live long and healthy lives. I am sure one could imagine that the old saying "a stitch in time saves nine" could be a true example, of how by taking care of one important aspect in our health plan, could save so many other issues along the way just waiting to catch its prey. It is so easy to ignore the little things and perhaps regret it later.

Another example could be the problem of a simple misunderstanding, becoming serious, due to miscommunication of an innocent comment. It is not too long before the whole situation can get completely out of hand! No one involved can see how this issue has developed, but rest assured that more than likely if not dealt with in the beginning, it could eventually snowball out of control. Unexplained, it can be left to fester like a boil under the skin, just waiting to burst open at the next provocation. So much hurt and pain caused by unresolved situations, whether real or imaginary, can lead to buried resentment and eventually anger. It must be worth dealing with any such like occasions straight away. Time is not on our side, when it comes to disputes and annoyances, and as such, it is not good to ignore them. I am sure there are so many more examples that could be mentioned, which by now you could think of yourself, especially when it comes to everyday living. Difficulties of this nature need timely action to remove them.

Maybe another anomaly that might be worth mentioning is do not put off until tomorrow, what you can do today. Procrastination is namely a word that means so much more under the surface. To some extent, I think it might have a similar meaning, although I have always thought of it as me trying to get out of something I am not keen to do. I think underlying my thinking, is if I leave it long enough it might not need to be done, or might not even be there to do next day. One could say that might be called dreaming, but to be honest what really happens is actually nothing. It is still there in the morning and 24 hours really, in everyday situations has not changed a thing. The only thing that has seemingly changed is the time and my mood, because I am now unhappy I had relied on my dreaming to delay the inevitable, namely whatever it was I was putting off doing is still there!

Perhaps, as we mature, the tendency to play this game with ourselves gradually lessons and we end up becoming more sensitive about procrastination. Maybe when we are young we do not bother too much about tomorrow, as we think we are immortal, so what is another day wasted delaying our plans. I think I can still remember those days; they always seemed longer and sunnier, than they do now and time passing, was given much less consideration because we thought then that it would never run out! We lived from one day to another, never realising how quickly the weeks and months were passing. Why should we care it was going to last for ever, or so we thought then and rightly so? We could not even think past the immediate. We were so busy enjoying the now, intertwined with long balmy evenings, we were made temporarily oblivious to tomorrow. Tricked into thinking that time stood still. Putting off until tomorrow was a way of life. The problem was then and still is, no matter how much we tell ourselves tomorrow will do, it actually will not because as time passes we will spend more and more time trying to catch up with it! You only have to speak to a member of the older generation to find that out. Just listen to what they say. 'I don't know where the time goes' is a favourite expression, and 'What ever happened to last week it just flew by'. What I think they are trying to say is that they do not manage to do the things they used to do with the same amount of time. Time has not changed, although to them it probably feels that way. The days seem more crowded because they are doing less, more likely than not, because they have slowed down. They cannot afford to put things aside until the next day because they would spend forever trying to catch up.

Time is not going to slow down its' pace to allow everything, frustrating as that can be, to be fitted in to an alternative time plan. At the end of the day, whether we want to admit it or not, we are the only thing that can change our schedule. We each have exactly 24 hours in a day, and it is up to us more often than not, as to how we live it, depending on the choices we make along the way.

Chapter 22

A Time to Die

Why can't we all live forever? Why does anyone have to die? We have all been there, I am sure, and these questions are probably the two most difficult and shattering questions to answer.

The realisation whilst growing up, that for reproduction to continue everything has to die, doesn't really help. Our first introduction to death, for most of us comes, with the death of our favourite animal or pet and it hurts. Sorting that out is bad enough, but even so, still doesn't answer the question. Death it seems, is ok so long as it's happening to others, but it is a different story when it is round about us! Too close up and personal is how I would put it, perhaps, not a comfortable place to be with one's own thoughts. Writing about death, has been a difficult choice for me, but it is an aspect of time that cannot be ignored.

I have come to realise as I have lost loved ones and special friends, as traumatic as that is to deal with, that there is a lot of fear of the unknown involved as well. How we deal with any fears is very individual and everyone reacts to dealing with it in different ways, but something we all have to acknowledge in this life, is that we are born and we will most certainly die. Knowing this, and in most cases not knowing when it could happen, is sometimes a cause for concern in all of us I am sure. Acceptance of any given situation, over which we have no control is always very difficult, so why should the question of death be any different? Living life as we know it, we are constantly reminded about it, and more closely affected when we lose those close to us. However, living in fear or obsessing about issues we have no control over is not healthy for anyone and perhaps, acceptance might more easily enable us to live a more fulfilled life without anxiety. To complicate things for each of us a little, there are those folk who teach that death is not the end, in fact it is the beginning. Others live this life, solely with the purpose of securing a place in the afterlife, or heaven as it is known by most.

There are also those who openly admit that they have no interest in any such things, stating categorically that when you are dead you are definitely without question dead, and there is nothing after that. Whatever doctrine we each choose to follow, there really is no one to ask, about what it's like to be dead and what to expect when it happens to us. Perhaps that's just as well, because I am sure, being human, we could all give our own slant on what we have experienced. Unfortunately, the fact is we have to die to find out. I suggest any doctrine we choose to follow requires a step of faith to believe we have made the right choice. Up to this moment in time, there are no trips to take, giving us a precursor of where we might end up. Different doctrines teach different outcomes, to passing on, we each have free choice as to which we wish to follow or believe in. Without doubt it is a highly emotive subject, which demands respect and sincerity and a great deal of understanding, for those who have ever been or are recently involved in the process of grieving. So long as it is out there, it is far enough away and we can deal with the moment and after a time move on, sooner or later the pain we are suffering will lesson and become more manageable.

We all have to die but most of us do not know when. I wonder if when we were born, we were given a date as to how long we would have to live, would it make us think and behave differently. Many lives throughout history, and even up to the present moment, have been destroyed with no thought of what it might have meant to the victims of such atrocities.

During the dark era of the Spanish Inquisition it has been revealed that more than 250,000 people were tortured and put to death, as a punishment for wanting to believe in a different religion or doctrine. This being ordered at the time, without so much as a second thought, by the perpetrators of such crimes! Death it seems is no respecter of persons, nor is it made easier to accept by knowing this. Perhaps, the only way to deal more easily with this fact is to endeavour to live everyday as if it were our last. That doesn't necessarily mean living as in doing, but more about living in the moment, perhaps being more appreciative and taking less for granted.

A quotation I read recently by G K Chesterton said, "The critical thing is whether you take things for granted or take them with gratitude". He was an English writer, poet and philosopher, as well as giving many other contributions to the literary world. It would seem by taking things with gratitude, and not so much for granted, doesn't leave much time to miss anything too much. Developing an awareness of our conscious state, should help us to look forward to the next beautiful moment, rather than living in the fear of losing it. Perhaps, the more we practice this, the greater chance we might have of cultivating a true moment by moment contentment. What a way to live without fear of what might happen in the future. Maybe it is up to each one of us to make it happen so that we might eventually be able to testify to the fact that 'Death has lost its sting!'

There have been many books written on another aspect of death and that is 'dying to self'. What does it really mean in the context of daily living? There are, it would appear many who would say, dying to self means putting our egos to death. In the first instance it would be fair to assume that without our egos we could not exist in this world. Some would say that our ego is the driving self, which has to survive above all else, no matter what might need to happen to do so. It seems the ego, is the survival part of our human nature, and is what develops the self-part of our personality. It would appear that it quite regularly wants its own way, so much so, even becoming unpopular is not a problem. Our ego can tell us that we can have whatever we want or choose, it really doesn't matter what it might cost us in terms of relationship, friendship or anything that might stand in our way. Taming the ego is a bit like trying to keep a wild head of hair under control, no sooner have you brushed it one way, it springs back to exactly the way it was, determined to do what it wants. Sometimes, no amount of time, pressure or effort seems to make any difference. It could be suggested, the ego could easily be in control of us, although it can be hard to see how at times. It's a big subject, and widely misunderstood, but for the sake of now I think it would be true to say it is our basic survival instincts at work. When threatened, it is survival at all costs, and can be undeniably forceful to get what it wants. The ego demands much and expects more than much, and depending on the circumstances surrounding its' development will be in constant need.

Time is what the ego lives on, the stronger the ego, the more time takes over your life. We are more often-than-not, driven by self, which will not stop till we get satisfaction. It could be described as a vicious circle which will never stop turning until we step out of it. In so doing, satisfying our own needs and wants will start to become second nature, being replaced by a sense of satisfaction and fulfilment which we didn't bargain on. As we give out so will we receive, finding a different new life which will become freer, where there was once stress, anxiety and constant demands. We could even find peace of mind with a simplicity beyond our understanding, and an enjoyment of life with a very different meaning and outcome, such as dying to self.

Chapter 23

Timeless Moments

What are timeless moments? Many would say they are moments that don't exist in time, in fact, they are time less. Others might say they have never thought about it, including those who might think that it's a really stupid question, why would you ever ask it in the first place? Asking questions that others might never think about, creates opportunities, to stop and wonder about life and what it is all about. Although for some, the answers to certain questions about life are difficult to answer, there must be those folk amongst us, who love to think about how and why life is the way it is. Appreciating the little things in life, which are here today and maybe gone tomorrow, could be just the way you might picture timeless moments. Timelessness is possibly being lost in time, which is more than likely for most of us, quite beyond our understanding. A sort of collection of moments all strung together like an exquisite string of pearls, precious and priceless, with a beauty that is only perceived by those who enter effortlessly into experiencing them. Of course, there would be some who could be forgiven for suggesting this is quite a strange way of thinking, and should they ask any learned scholar, could be proven to be totally right in their suggestion. However, it has to be said any experience is generally interpreted differently by every individual.

I used to think that timeless moments were those times that had no end and therefore would just go on and on, but of course that couldn't possibly be true, because time doesn't stand still and nor could it. The very essence of time is, it has to go on and keep running, or life as we know it would come to an end. The word timeless would suggest that there was no measure of time, and that even if we were to try to measure it, it would be impossible. Perhaps the word moments might give a better understanding of what timeless might mean. For me moments are those occurrences, which happen in a blink of an eye, or a flash of lightening, or a thought, which could be gone in a second. The speed at which they come and are gone is not humanly possible to measure in our understanding. To think of a moment, as anything more than a minute or two, would be too long to call it a moment. It could be described as, a bit like trying to take a photo of a moving object, which is almost impossible to do for most of us.

Perhaps timeless moments are an illusion, like watching a beautiful sunset, which at the time, feels as if it will never stop. The change we are seeing is so subtle, as we are transfixed on the beauty it creates around it, we can become oblivious to what is actually happening. The sun is actually disappearing in front of our eyes and it will only be a short time before it is completely gone from view. Somehow, we have managed to fool ourselves into thinking that what we are seeing, is going to be there for however long we stand watching it. The fact is, it is not the case, and what seemed like a timeless moment has actually passed. Somehow, being involved in the very experience of seeing something so beautiful taking place, only to be gone is what makes it timeless.

Can we ever capture timeless moments on camera or see them in books? Almost surely not when you consider the many timeless moments throughout life, especially when children are growing up, which are impossible to put into storage so to speak. The very fact that they happened in front of our eyes, we were so involved in the happenings at the time, it was impossible to recreate them. Even so, wanting to register them in our minds forever, was never possible to because they were in transit and changing every second. Sometimes, it would seem it is difficult to capture those moments, even in our memories. As fast as we are processing the moment, it is gone and the next moment starts processing itself, too quickly for the brain to register. I believe it is true to say we tend to probably remember incidences or happenings, as we interpret them at the time as an outsider of the moment, rather than being in the moment and actually living in it. That itself creates a different dimension, one that is never stationary, but none the less very real. It is as though we are part of an experience that is creating itself around us, which we are participating in, all be it sometimes as an onlooker.

I wonder is it possible to create timeless moments ourselves? I am not sure about this only to say that there have been times, when I have been involved in creating time and space, for what have turned out eventually to be seemingly timeless moments. I am left wondering, if those moments would have happened, if the time and space had not been put aside. Perhaps not, but I think it is true to say that the outcome was not planned or anticipated, and therefore completely unexpected. Perhaps what makes moments timeless is the very fact that they are not expected or anticipated. Because of that, we are actually able to be in the moment and experience a type of timelessness, which is difficult or almost impossible to create ourselves. We are unable to resist these moments, because we are involved in them as a participant, just because we are there. We are a prisoner of the experience, unable to tear ourselves away from what we might think, or want to happen. It is as though the moment is in charge, it controls us, only to disappear when it is over, leaving us mesmerised.

Whatever the reasons, or however they happen I am glad timeless moments exist. I dare to hope that everyone has had, or will have an opportunity to experience such times, and as such, our lives will be enriched by them every day.

Chapter 24

A Time to Love

"In essentials unity, in non-essentials liberty: and in all things love". It took me a while to think about this quotation from Tolstoy's book relating to his life, but it was the 'and in all things love', that really bothered me the most. Love comes in many forms, and I do not want to be repetitive about something that I am sure could have been said hundreds of times, but I wanted to make sense of this statement in the cold light of day. It is all very well to say 'Love in all things' but can we actually do this? I am sure we can all say the words and truly believe we mean them, because most of us want to do just that, but in reality is a different matter. It is easy to love a friend, because a friend is of our own choosing, but the opposite. In the past, I have reconciled my conscience, by trying to prefer not to hate anyone. I thought this would be a compromise. You may have other ideas, and rightly so, but is it enough? Perhaps, just a few of us are in the right place to take hold of the true meaning of love your enemy, as much as we might want to be.

Are we truly prepared to still love when it really hurts? Maybe, but I fear not very often, because perhaps love costs more than we are prepared to give or can justify. Where can we draw the line if at all? Speaking from my own experience, as I am sure you would only be prepared to do yourself, it does bare thinking about. My instincts tell me life without love would be unbearable and impossible. Love forgives like no other and where there is no forgiveness, a deep recurring ache can linger within, which is hard to live with, in fact, it can turn to bitterness. The only problem with that is, bitterness only ends up hurting us, in ways that we cannot imagine at the time. I am certain love is able to deal with this, when we give it time, and can change many otherwise immovable attitudes in life.

In fantasy we can be led to believe, romantic love rarely works out and is more than likely to fail, ending up disappearing from the picture altogether. Is it therefore crazy to believe or trust in such things! I believe that Eros love is very real, and romance is what helps to keep love alive, when all else seems like it has been raging against it. Endless pressures of comparisons from the media, gossip columns, and magazines would like to have us believe that romance is the last thing needed on the agenda. I think differently. I believe both men and women thrive on it, and that special touch and loving attention, is vital in our everyday relationships. If the love of your life hasn't time to make you feel special, who can? I believe the secret to good romance, is giving time to think about it, or actually making it happen.

Can we love beyond reason? Firstly, what is reason? Each individual, has a sense of reason, which is their own? Comparing is likely to be futile, as reason is ones' own ability to decipher thoughts and feelings, mainly based on experience. To pass judgement on another's sense of reason would be more than likely based on ignorance. How can anyone know another's willingness to love, beyond what we in our own minds and emotions, might be prepared to do. We all have a different story to consider. In the historical event and love story between Mark Anthony and Cleopatra, their deaths, were due to an undying love, which some might think superseded all reason? Whatever we think, this story has been repeated in so many places and so many ways via books, and films with great success. If the story is factual, perhaps it could be that love outweighed reason. Some could think Mark Anthony's actions of killing himself on hearing of Cleopatra's death, was complete and utter madness, although others might be able to see the power behind the love they shared. Either way, many millions of pounds have been the result, of exploiting one of the greatest love stories ever told. How many would be prepared to die for the one they love today? I suppose, that is an unanswerable question, depending on the circumstances we might find ourselves in at the time. Even so, the power of love has been expressed in many a newspaper or magazine, when a life has been given to save another.

Time to love others is not always as available as many would like, as no doubt by those who have to make do could feel, with whatever might come their way. Love can be in short supply for many and many social problems could be the result of exactly that. A lack of time, money, busyness and ambition, to name but a few, takes priority over the need to spend time with the ones we love. There is little compensation for the unhappiness resulting from this, at least not for long! The media can try to trick us into thinking, by accumulating things, our happiness will increase, but I do not see evidence of that around me. People's open expression of anger, frustration, impatience etc. is giving a different picture. Relationships especially, suffer in many ways, when there is not enough time for love and affection. One only has to read the papers or watch the news, to see that having everything as some famous film stars etc. appear to have, does not bring happiness for long as the divorces we hear about prove.

Children especially, can be seen as a burden rather than a pleasure to love, and it seems this can be in epidemic proportions if we are to believe what the statistics tell us almost daily. Time given to love and affection is a sacrifice made which is difficult to ask for or insist upon, when you are a babe in arms, only interested in where your next meal is coming from. We as the nurturing adults have a responsibility to provide it without question, but at best, we can only hope to give away what we know and have experienced for ourselves. Good parenting for our offspring is not instinctive, as some would want us to believe, it is more probable we more easily give, what we have received in this instance.

Profound as this might be, the human race survives, but perhaps a more appropriate description might be the word 'exists'. Unfortunately, the bad effects from a lack of love can be around for a long time, with guidance and tender, loving care it is hoped the bad effects will one day be reversed.

Chapter 25

Giving Time to Sex

S ex is one of the shorter words in the English Dictionary, but even so possibly one of the most powerful, for so many reasons. Sex has endured the test of time down through the ages, and although there is nothing to compare with its tenacity, it is constantly challenged and those who pursue it can still be found wanting.

As it is well known, animals participate in sex at a very basic level and maybe enjoy it to some degree or other. However, if I remember correctly from my biology lessons from long past, the participation was a necessary act for the procreation of the species. Animalistic sex does appear to look a bit that way, but how can we assume pleasure does not exist? You see mothers such as lions or elephants so attached to their young, especially immediately after birth, and for some months afterwards. The nurturing behaviour is amazing to watch, and probably expressed by most of the species, except perhaps the very lowest form of life. I guess, without this innate instinct, the survival of certain species would probably very soon end. Interestingly enough there are those humans amongst us, who believe that the human sexual act is also purely for procreation, but maybe this subject should be for another day.

It seems that the subject of sex evokes many extreme reactions, some totally devoid of feeling and some quite the opposite. It has been responsible for making individuals crazy for the act itself, to the point of addiction in order to satisfy an insatiable deep need, and others so disinterested they enjoy eating chocolate or watching football more, or somewhere in-between. It is probably, one of the biggest ways of making money, the world has ever known. Since the Victorian era, the adult sex industry has flourished tremendously, especially since the introduction of the internet, pornography being one of the most popular, or so it appears. However, it is portrayed there is no stopping it. Unfortunately, the growing problem, which needed considering before it happened, is how easy it is now for the younger generation to be involved all be it inadvertently! Sex shops, sex toys and the blatant advertising of such in magazines and newspapers, are there for all ages to see with seemingly no thought of the outcome. The provocative question now is how to deal with this ever-increasing potential problem and the consequences of it. According to recent statistics in the media, there are now serious concerns about child rape by children as young as 11 years old. Exposure to such material at such a young age, must have unforeseen disadvantages, to the developing minds and emotions of those not old enough to understand. One would like to believe, there are more than a few concerned adults out there who are taking action, although the quotation 'shutting the stable door after the horse has bolted' springs to mind.

There are many different attitudes and approaches to sex and none of us is really in a position to judge or say which is right or wrong. However, I would like to highlight a point of view in the context of this book. Do you give time to sex? Please note, at this point I did not say, do you give time for sex? I believe there is a subtle difference. Firstly, anyone at any time, can have sex, the only hesitation there might be is to find another person who might want to join in with that wish. The media would have us believe that it is not difficult. All it requires is a place to do it and 2 consenting adults. Somewhat simplified you might say, but that is exactly why it is called time for sex. However, it is an activity shared by a mutual other significant or not, it would appear it does not really matter the result is the same, sex happens or not.

To my mind, there is nothing to compare with the deep intimacy, longing and excitement created by the mystery of one of the most beautiful expressions of love and life. Sex can be divine or just another act like cleaning your teeth, it is what you make it, processed or created. Processed is easy and probably short-lived, it requires very little planning or emotional investment 'Wham Bam thank you Mam', but created that is another story. Most of us are lucky enough to have a choice. I would like to suggest that giving time to sex has a somewhat different meaning. I believe the sex act is an art, a gift in the making. As all artistic involvements, it requires time, creativity and imagination, not to mention passion. I would even dare to suggest that time spent in thought, preparation and creating opportunities for the old-fashioned word romance could be positively rewarding. Of course, spontaneous sex is wonderful and exciting and adds spice to an already delicious meal. However, let us face it; if we had fast food takeaways every day, I am sure we would soon be looking elsewhere for alternatives, to supplement out diet. Boredom would eventually need replacing, with newfound greener pastures to graze upon, if we are to consider current trends. Websites created for making new excitement, the only criteria required for membership, is you need to be married! What does that say about the subject?

No, I believe like all good nutritious, lovingly prepared meals there needs to be a little forward planning, thought provoking creativity and time spent on savouring every mouthful when you eventually settle down to eat. What about atmosphere or ambience, surely that has to be an all-important part of the experience, to heighten the senses. Would you eat a beautifully prepared meal off the floor or standing up? I do not think so. It would definitely devalue the effort made, and undermine the care and attention given to making this delicacy. My point is why should giving time to sex be any different? I believe we might ignore or overlook the importance of this at our peril.

When we create opportunities for giving time to sex, we can increase excitement and the intensity of desire, far beyond what we could imagine.

Magical moments might happen in love stories or in films or books, but may never happen in reality, if no one puts the ingredients together in the first place. Lust is short lived. Passion is from the heart, and builds long lasting physical pleasure, heightened by desire and longing. Giving and receiving in equal measure, action feeding off reaction. An enjoyment of sexual pleasure difficult to describe in words, as there are none that adequately expresses the depth of feeling experienced. Time stands still, as increasing pleasures eventually bring you to a place of mutual fulfilment and satisfaction. Why would we not want to nurture such an amazing sense of belonging, joy and oneness with those we have chosen to be our life partners? Like all things, we value, I believe we also need to give our time to creating exquisite sex, based on love, trust and intimacy. How long it takes to develop is as I see it not so important, but maybe we owe it to ourselves and to our significant other to spend time nurturing what could be one of the most precious experiences we can ever have in life.

Think about it, if you are not happy to miss out in this area of your life, then perhaps it is up to you to make sure it does not happen. Everything in life it seems, which is worth hanging on to, requires effort, enthusiasm, and time to grow and develop. Why should sex be any different? Intimacy does not just happen; it flourishes when two people connect at a level, of feelings built on mutual trust and desire, with actions of giving and receiving rolling off each other like the recurrent waves on the seashore. As each wave hits the shore, so another is building right behind it in a never-ending pattern, until it ends for whatever reason. The fulfilment and pleasure created by such experiences entice more of the same, which could eventually become effortless in the making. Any feelings of vulnerability become a distant memory. Ageing is impossible because time stands still as you live in these moments of completeness and oneness. If any problems exist then surely it would be crazy to ignore them and not seek professional help or engage in mutual sharing to find a way to resolve them. We are all entitled to give and receive enjoyment and pleasure even though there are times I am sure, when we feel unworthy of such things. Sometimes, looking outside the box and encouraging our partners by our attention and love can build bridges and create the ability to overcome negative feelings, about our or their possible feeling of unworthiness. Sexual compatibility takes time to develop and once realised, requires our thoughts as well as actions to enjoy it to the full. Time given towards creating such experiences will be mutually built upon gradually, a rare treasure to give away, and then to be returned.

Chapter 26

A Time to Lose

Nelson Mandela once wrote "Time gives back to us those things we have lost, in wisdom and memories" and I remember when I read it, I had to keep turning the implications of those words over in my mind. I decided that I needed to understand what he was trying to say and after a while, I managed to grasp the meaning of what those words might have meant for me and of course, they will remain in my heart. Later however, I also realised that generally speaking we have all lost many things in our lives and we have probably struggled to make sense of it, especially when it has meant learning to live without those we love. For each of us this will hold a different story and only time can heal the pain, but how much better to think that even though we have lost, even so through it we might have also gained. Precious memories spring to mind and perhaps after a while, we might start to nurture the wisdom taught, even though we may not have realised it at the time.

I am sure there is nothing, at the time that could help us to understand what exactly was happening and why, especially when it is relating to the loss of a loved one. The pain it creates in our hearts and lives is so overwhelming; it can be consuming. No one could ever predict our individual reaction to such, nor could they know how long it might last. We struggle to make sense of many things in life but this kind of loss is the most difficult. Even when our loss, is of someone who is very old and you know that losing them is inevitable, we still try to hang on to them rather than allow ourselves to let them go. Deep love and affection and many dear memories are significant to that person which, at the time, we think we will probably lose those as well, but of course, that is not true. In the immediate moment, repetitious thoughts take over our minds, almost relentlessly, darting from one event to another that we might have shared with our loved one and how we might have done things differently or not. Despite our efforts to concentrate on other things, sleep can evade us for hours, as we relive recent memories and last moments spent together. We are all very different and react to loss in many different and personal ways, but one thing that is common to all is the fact, that time is a great healer. Whether it is by days, weeks, months or years, we trust we will eventually be able to think about our loved one without pain.

Is there a right time to lose? I would say 'never'. It creates an empty hole within us which we are convinced, will never be filled, by anything or anyone. So often, all we can see is darkness and emptiness where once there was light and a feeling of belonging. The 'why' questions never stop coming; like an irritating, dripping tap that we cannot turn off. Tears of laughter have turned to tears of sadness and pain, and tomorrow is a day to look forward to. For some joy does come in the morning, but for many that is a long time coming, and for some it never comes.

Our experience of loss will never be the same as anyone else, and to think it could be possible is unthinkable. We struggle through the long dark hours of days, and nights, exhausting ourselves trying to understand what has happened, and after brief intervals of total numbness we start all over again, eventually when all else has failed hopefully acceptance comes.

Is there anything in the world that can make this part of our journey easier? In all honesty, I would say not. Having a positive outlook definitely helps, but in time of so much grief, it is a struggle. Those around us cannot possibly understand the pain we are suffering, as they can only own their own. We can feel like an island, completely alone, sometimes feeling suffocated by the strong tides of pain that wash up over us, only to subside and resurface when we least expect them.

However, on a lighter more positive note, most of us do survive and the sun does shine again and we can start to look forward to tomorrow again. Slowly from the depths of sorrow, our hearts gradually fill with joy and we are not afraid to laugh again. We manage to store our fond memories where no one else can find them to remind ourselves of the precious moments spent with our loved ones, only to return them to the secret place in our hearts. No one promised this journey of life would be easy, and many times, it can be tough, but overall we owe it to ourselves to move on from difficult times. Who knows how long or where our journey may take us. One thing however is very true; we are not alone. Everyone who has ever lived has or will experience loss, whether they want to or not. What makes the difference in our lives is how we each react and deal with it.

Loss comes in many ways, not only in losing a loved one. I dare to say that the extent of our loss we can probably only measure by our attachment to what it represents, which means we could lose a friend or a job and depending on what it meant to us, we will react or grieve accordingly. Our attachment to things or objects is a good deal of sentimentality, but none the less means a lot to the owner. Pets come at a high premium when you consider the relationship that can develop between them and their owners. I am sure nothing can prepare someone, who has enjoyed the company of a beloved dog or cat or even a horse, for the emptiness that ensues when they are no longer around. Even though we all accept that death is part of life, it can still leave a gaping hole that is hard to fill.

Loss also comes in many shapes and sizes and has a different meaning to each one. It is more than likely only when you lose something, you realise how much you appreciated it. It is ironical to think that it sometimes takes loss to happen, before the reality of what we once had comes to our notice. The pace of life is such that we can take so much for granted, only to find that it could be irreplaceable once gone. If only we had taken a bit more time to appreciate what we had before we lost it. What does it take to come to this realisation before it is too late? Is there anything in life that can prepare us for the inevitability of these moments?

I often wonder if there is anything, other than the experience of loss, which could give us even a brief insight before it happens. Is it possible to educate our children about something so difficult to accept in our own lives, let alone in theirs? I sense that the reality of loss for children, is more easily overcome, by something else more relevant at the time, such as their basic needs, which if not met can be traumatic for all. Their pain is difficult to understand and empathise with. Perhaps we will never know how much damage, has been done in their innocent little lives and the scars that may result. Perhaps it is only in adulthood that we are able to process the loss we have experienced as children and in many cases, I am sure it does not really make a lot of sense to us at the time. Trying to piece together the past and the present can often be difficult to do even when we dedicate time to it. Fortunately, for the human race we are very resilient to pain and suffering and with love and understanding we can recover as much as we are able.

Turning negatives into positives is easier said than done, but to be sure when achieved it makes us that much stronger and able to cope with any future losses which we may have to face. As has been said many times before, time is a great healer. As such, it is sometimes all we have to rely on, to help us to recover from those times that we feel like we are walking through quick sand. Every step seemingly harder than the one before. Turning loss into gain is difficult indeed, but it is not impossible and there are many stories throughout history where people have testified to this fact. These stories give each of us courage to pursue a positive answer for ourselves, however long it might take. Even so, we have to want to do just that whatever it might cost, the choice is ours to make.

Chapter 27

Only a Matter of Time.

Superfluous is a word that springs to mind, when you consider how many people might be feeling at this moment, or possibly every day. They may feel life continues, irrespective of whether they are here or not, a painful truth. Being more than is wanted, desired or needed could be a regular experience for many, but why is this? Being surplus to requirements, is a cruel game that is played, when people are no longer regarded as having any useful purpose. In fact, there is always someone else who can take their place at any given time; whether in work or in the family or in relationships. At work it is to be expected, no one wants to work for ever, but family, friends and relationships, well that hurts! Are people really so replaceable? One always tries to think that cannot be true, but I am not so sure anymore. There is a time and a place for everything, they say and if it has little or no use, then throw it away. It is commonly accepted that we are living in a throwaway society these days. Everything can so easily be replaced. Surely not people you think, how can that be? Well it's really easy; it all comes down to priorities. It is said that familiarity breeds contempt; sad but true!

Maybe life is too stressful, so everything is regarded as either too much trouble, or not important enough that it's worth troubling over. Many of us can be so busy that nothing is noted, understood or regarded as that important when it comes to giving our time. We can become quite indifferent to everything especially other people. It begs the question why? The truth is, it is probably completely unintentional and the effects it has on others not obvious, only to those being ignored or overlooked. In the busy scheme of life as we know it, people are in existence but not really there, unless of course they make loud noises to make sure they are heard. Maybe as time passes those around us become more like pieces of old furniture, made to fit where they stand, worn out by frequent use but too familiar to get rid of; either way surplus to requirements and past their sell by date. The only real difference between humans and a piece of furniture is furniture has no feelings.

Feeling superfluous after leading an active and interesting life can only be imagined for some of us, but for others it is a fact of life. Each day that passes, is one more day to live in the past for some, rather than to think there is anything available for the future. Fear of being no longer needed, for whatever reason, must be a reality for so many whose lives are no longer being lived with purpose. Loneliness for many, must be a daily nightmare to be lived day and night, with seemingly no respite. In this situation, the inevitability of losing interest and motivation must be terrifying. Learning to live with only oneself, when life was full and meaningful, or when it was shared by a lifelong partner who has passed on, can only be dreaded. Failing eyesight or hearing, or just simply lack of mobility, must create levels of frustration and anxiety almost unbearable to live with. Aimlessly wandering about the shops when mobility allows, not really paying attention to what is happening around you, or speaking to anyone in particular must be so difficult. It would seem, that one of the growing problems in our society today, is the fate of those who live alone. They must often feel that no one cares or even knows. Logically, how could they? They are not likely to broadcast the fact, for fear of being thought of as inadequate, or sad. Well, perhaps that is absolutely the case, and in time it could happen to anyone of us. Maybe it is good that we do not know the future, because it may be that we could not face the thought of such, if it meant being so alone with no useful purpose!

Where is all this heading, you might think, perhaps, in an intolerant manner? Honestly, absolutely nowhere, because it will mean nothing to most people and very little to those who are left. Why mention it then? Perhaps because, it is only when something is gone, you will probably find you miss it the most, only to discover that it is more than likely irreplaceable. On the other hand, there may be many times in life when you lose something and are lucky enough to find it again. However, it may be too late to make any difference, because by then, perhaps what was lost may have been replaced or forgotten about. If only someone had brought these matters to your attention sooner it may have changed the outcome? It would be sad to think, we could get into a situation in life where because of lack of time, we were riddled with guilt or shame. Feelings of wishing we had paid more attention to detail, when it came to loved ones, especially our elderly loved ones. Each of us has every good intention, but time passes so quickly because life is so busy, it is understandable we could so easily forget our good intentions and end up doing nothing. To realise we have failed someone we love, in terms of giving up just a small amount of our time for them, whether it be to take them out or just to sit and idly chat together, could negatively influence our fond memories. I guess one thing that may help us to avoid such a feeling, might be to come to realise, that one day we could be in a similar situation; all be it in a different place in time, with different circumstances, but none the less on our journey through life it could eventually become inevitable.

There are times when I think about the modern society in which we live today, and I can see many areas where I feel we fail each other, because of lack of time and displaced priorities. I hope we will not forget to empathise with those who feel they don't have much to offer, because our whole existence does not just depend on financial success and being accepted for such. If we should lose the desire to care and show love and respect, by investing precious time in others, it will only be a matter of time before we also lose an important ingredient of life itself. The core of our society, upon which our family life is built and is dependent, will disintegrate and become non-existent. Community spirit, is built upon individuals and families giving of themselves and their time, in order to share the burdens that the less fortunate have to deal with on a daily basis. The fabric of our society cannot survive without them and I am sure none of us realise, until it's too late, how very precious our contribution is and will be in years to come.

In less materialistic societies, community living is paramount for their survival, to support and nurture those in need. Families rely on local gatherings such as weddings and celebrations, where they can support and share each other's burdens, which can be their only source of help and support. Sharing is another basic component of living within a structured society, where food and nutrition are given away without question, to those amongst them who are unable to fend for themselves. I am sure, they have their fair share of fallings out and differences, but on the whole survival is a shared burden by all. Living in such an environment must require great patience, unselfishness and compassion. When those around become fragile and vulnerable, neither of which is possible to avoid in life, must be so much harder without love and support from those close family and community ties. In these different cultures across the world elderly are revered and respected and it is an honour for the family to give back time to those who have given them life. It would be unthinkable and absolutely unacceptable not to do this! It is a principle of life that ensures the continuation of the core of the society in which they live and die. Sharing and caring, maintains life in tortuous situations, which in our Western Society we can hardly imagine. We only have to look at what is going on in the world around us to see the facts for ourselves.

Sadly, I think over time the future of our village community life as it once was, is under threat of being disconnected and neglected, through a growing lack of time and interest in the lives of those around us. Modern family life is already struggling to cope with the need to keep up with paying the bills and the outgoings. Just trying to keep up with the demands that are being placed on it are colossal, creating its' own difficulties upon the nuclear family too. The dangers are, as in all areas of life that end up being neglected, it will be almost impossible to withstand outside forces of destruction and chaos. Strength has to come from within in order to sustain everyone's usefulness and purpose, no matter what their age or experience. Being part of that must give a sense of belonging and an eagerness to be involved. Why, because of age or situation should anyone be excluded in the scheme of life, when they have so much to offer all be it big or small? No one needs to be lonely or unnoticed, when there is a willingness to communicate with each other, regardless of the time it costs. Certainly, most definitely, no-one needs to ever feel superfluous to requirements, no matter what their age or status. Maybe we should all do a rethink regarding our current lifestyles and our order of priorities within them.

Chapter 28

Is it time to take action?

How long can we make excuses, for our indifference to what is happening, in our lives and in the world around us? There are so many reasons, too many to list here, but maybe to mention a few common ones might be of some interest. It has been said that indifference is worse than love or hate; why is that? I believe it is because it is neither hot nor cold, which means that it could well cause us not to react when perhaps we might, especially on some important issues, hence the term indifference.

There is the analogy of the frog and its' destiny. The saying goes, that if you were to place a frog into boiling water, if would instantly jump out to rescue itself. However, if you placed the frog into cold to tepid water and slowly heat the water to boiling, the frog would be oblivious to what was happening to the change in the temperature. Consequently, it would probably stay where it was and of course, eventually die! In other words, a growing indifference through desensitisation can cause us to be oblivious to those things around us, which could really benefit from our attention. We can get so familiar with the current situation around us, it can cause us to be immobilised, and thus out of action. Indifference or desensitisation, is like an insipid poison slowly and subtly causing us to be ineffective, demotivated, non-communicative and even disinterested in those situations around us in everyday life, and also in the world. Even though we may not have noticed it happening, it can affect us all, in very many different ways. The problem is because it is slow growing, it is a bit like the example of the frog in the lukewarm water, it can lull us into a false sense of security and indifference.

What is actually happening to us? I will try to give some examples below. One example of indifference, can develop when you take pain killers or drink alcohol, on a very regular basis. Eventually it will need more of the same, to produce a similar effect as to when they were started. What has happened here to cause this development? It is caused, by the body slowly getting used to the dosage and accommodating it, to the extent that it becomes used to the initial amount of drugs or alcohol and requires more of the same for a similar effect. This in medical circles is known as desensitisation.

Desensitisation, resulting in indifference can happen in many forms. Violence is one area in particular, where humans are able to adapt to more and more serious scenes of violence, which will gradually produce an increasing amount of non-reaction to that which is being watched or experienced. It has to be said that violence of any form, whether to humans or animals, is sickening. Over the years, the opportunity to watch films during which an increasing amount of violence is being portrayed, has become more and more prevalent, becoming almost impossible to monitor. Looking back in history, it was considered the norm for crowds to gather, to watch horrendous acts of violence towards fellow human beings. Stories of hangings and public atrocities were an afternoons entertainment. Perhaps, the attendance was ordered by those in control, to substantiate their positions of power over those who were in less fortunate, vulnerable situations. Controlling the masses, by instilling fear into their hearts, I am sure had a profound effect in producing a deep level of subservience. The same has been recorded about the horrifying treatment and torture and worse, from those in positions of power, even within the church during the time of the Spanish Inquisition. Is it any wonder those who were forced to watch such things, sooner or later had to develop some form of emotional detachment? It had to be a form of protection, in order to not be affected so deeply, by what they were experiencing in front of their eyes!!

With the inevitable indifference from the developing desensitisation to violence, in whatever form, the question needs to be asked where will it all end? It needs to be asked, what is an acceptable level of violence to which our children can be exposed, before it starts to have an irreversible effect on their minds? Their minds still in the early stages of development, how will it come to affect their behaviour as adults, and if so to what degree? Such exposure, could diminish their developing sensitivity over time, and thus any perceived responsibility or restraints to act or react to such scenes, real or imaginary. To my mind desensitisation and therefore, developing indifference speaks for itself, the dangers are obvious. As I see it, we each have an individual and collective responsibility, to make choices to protect young minds who are the generation of tomorrow.

Domestic violence is arguably on the increase, if one is to believe the statistics displayed in the media, through TV programmes and tabloids. Some women walk in fear of being attacked, for whatever reason particularly in family situations, especially behind closed doors. Apparently it is said that one woman a week or more is killed by domestic violence and the figures are not diminishing. One could argue that 200 years ago, women were also battered to death on a regular basis, but I am not sure there are any reliable statistics or recordings about such things. The only reason I mention it, is because to some extent the attitude is, that women who are battered are partly at fault, because they go back to the perpetrator of the violence they suffer. However, it could also be an example, of a growing indifference or desensitisation to the pain and fear they are suffering. Trying to cope with an increasing hopeless cycle of abuse, and the inevitable inability to do anything about it the longer it goes on, must be intolerable and completely unmanageable. Sadly, however it just makes the whole situation worse, as statistics can prove.

Sexual desensitisation, leading to indifference is a topic that few people would perhaps be aware of, or want to acknowledge. The consequences are endless and could be long term, if we were to just stop to think about it. There is big money in the sex industry at a cost to many which is not only financial. Pornography can not only become a form of addiction, but also desensitisation can easily be an added problem, which can leave its own difficulties to deal with. This can subtly develop without anyone noticing. until symptoms start to develop such as a dissatisfied, individual response to sex in the reality of everyday life, and perhaps a growing inability to be fulfilled in one's own relationships.

Following porn sites on a regular basis does not require any emotional input, so any time spent watching them can bring excitement for a while, without the possibility of ending in disappointment. Over time however, emotional detachment can easily develop and could continue into reality, sometimes creating difficulties when trying to sustain a loving relationship. To be sure the newspapers, magazines, and agony columns bear witness to it, when broken relationships are the main focus we read about. It would not be right to blame any one issue in particular, as there must be numerous issues for relationship breakdowns. Suffice to say however, it is not rocket science to reason if you work in a sweet shop, after a length of time one could easily develop an addiction to sweets. Worse still, if you eat enough of them whenever you feel like it, it won't be long before you will become dissatisfied with the choices around you. Then you might well feel the need to look elsewhere to find new flavours, even so, inevitably the choices will run out and what then? Many argue, that the sexual freedom displayed in almost every scenario you can think about, especially in advertising today, is healthy and necessary. However, I think there is another outcome which could develop. Eventually, boredom or comparisons are going to be made, resulting in streams of mistrust, possible betrayal and desensitisation to follow, the statistics of which speak for themselves.

I think it's true to say that indifference could also immobilize us to do anything much about those areas of our lives and ourselves, that in the future could turn out to be important to us. Perhaps, with the everyday stress levels of living in this age today, our priorities can become confused and misleading. What was important once is almost phased out, like hiding documents on a computer, or blurred vision when we need glasses. Perhaps lack of time is becoming a form of desensitisation, as we become less and less aware of how little time we spend sharing, talking and loving those important significant others in our lives. We can become addicted to stress, like anything else and it can blind us to issues which are the building blocks of life itself.

Should we not 'Wake up and Smell the Roses' once and for all? At least limit the damage that desensitisation and developing indifference can bring? I believe in the saying, 'Better late than never' so why not stop and ask the question. Has indifference, in the form of desensitisation taken a hold of my life and if so, should I not re-evaluate my thinking and perhaps take action, before it is too late to change it?

Conclusion

The time it has taken you to read this book can only be measured in minutes, or maybe hours. More importantly, are the possible consequences of reading it in the first place. Perhaps what you have read has made no difference to your thinking, or maybe it has prompted you to consider the many facets of your own life, which up to now you may not have concerned you at all.

In most cases, I hope it will have helped to bring you to a place of mindfulness, and a desire to spend more time becoming aware of your own understanding. Self-awareness is a powerful tool, which when used wisely, can bring freedom of choice sometimes left undetected for a lifetime.

Our very existence, is time being lived on a daily basis, however long that might be. Surely we owe it to ourselves to spend some of the time allotted to each of us, in finding out how best not to regret a single minute of our passing through it, by avoiding self-discovery.

There are those who believe you cannot argue with Destiny, maybe that is true, but I am one who believes that you can change the way you approach it if you choose too. The only requirement is the desire to do just that.

Enjoy your journey.

Lightning Source UK Ltd.
Milton Keynes UK
UKHW040049080219
336901UK00001B/90/P